Psychotherapy Tales

Psychotherapy Tales

The Making of a Family Therapist

Aldo Gurgone

Wisdom Moon Publishing
2018

PSYCHOTHERAPY TALES

THE MAKING OF A FAMILY THERAPIST

Copyright © 2018 Wisdom Moon Publishing LLC

Published by Wisdom Moon Publishing LLC
San Diego, CA, USA

Wisdom Moon™, the Wisdom Moon logo™, *Wisdom Moon Publishing*™, and *WMP*™ are trademarks of Wisdom Moon Publishing LLC.

www.WisdomMoonPublishing.com

ISBN 978-1-938459-69-6 (softcover, alk. paper)
ISBN 978-1-938459-72-6 (eBook)

LCCN 2018959005

Table of Contents

Foreword

Aldo Gurgone has been doing psychotherapy for over 45 years and this book is a pearl of wisdom and humanity in dealing with individuals' dysfunctions, as well as family life difficulties and conflicts. The title *Psychotherapy Tales: The Making of a Family Therapist* reflects fully what is in the book: ten chapters with the description of a therapeutic story in each of them. The issues presented are very challenging and varied: from long-term hospitalized psychotic adult patients, to bulimic or suicidal adolescents, to grief and loss in the family, as well as multicultural couple and family dilemmas.

The link between these stories is Aldo himself, who is the main and only therapist engaged in all these therapeutic encounters. In each of the stories, Aldo has chosen to take a position of humility and authenticity, in contrast to the magic and glamour, or even the mystery that often shrouds the therapeutic relationship. In this sense, through the different tales, we can see an active therapist who is fully committed (head and heart) to help his patients to elicit their greatest resources, and his ability to attune to individual and family pain and suffering, and to guide them toward healthy and fulfilling solutions.

Aldo demonstrates many skills, among them a great sense of humour and creativity (see the long fairy tale he wrote in dealing with a six-year-old girl and her mother, or the use of the biblical metaphor "Jesus travelled through the desert" to help a dehydrated patient drink water) and a variety of techniques from the use of paradoxical injunction to the exploration of the family genogram and the preparation of family rituals to heal grief and loss.

Aldo doesn't like to describe the theory that guides his therapy, but his method of work is implicit and comprehensive when you carefully read his tales. The sub-title, *The Making of a Family Therapist*, clearly demonstrates Aldo's development as a therapist and his focus on the broader context in which the individual lives. He always has the family in mind, even when he meets individual clients, and occasionally he enlarges the dual setting, inviting a key member of the family for a special meeting. Aldo has a three-generational, systemic map of the family in his mindset, which is especially useful when he deals with conflicts and cultural diversities and loyalties transmitted through generations.

He is comfortable in working in a hospital ward or in his consulting room, as well as in home visiting. He has the wonderful ability (which is not often present), to learn from his own mistakes. For example, he experimented and found that certain metaphors can work with a client in a specific context, but that they are useless if repeated in other situations.

Using Dante's metaphor in the *Divine Comedy*, in his introduction Aldo describes his move from *Hell* (studying law) to *Paradise*: becoming a Psychotherapist. This image gives the sense of a profession which is also very enriching for us therapists if we are able to show humanity and accept the lessons of life from the people who choose to share the most intimate and vulnerable part of themselves with us in therapy.

Maurizio Andolfi, MD
Master Family Therapist

Preface

"Lose all hope, ye that enter..." These are early lines of Dante Alighieri's classic, *The Divine Comedy*. These words were written at the entrance to a cave leading to Hell. As a student of Italian Literature, I studied this classic text, which was divided into three parts: Hell, Purgatory, and Paradise. In many ways, my academic and professional life has reflected this journey, especially entering the Hell at university, when I initially enrolled to study Law. As with Dante's classic, Hell is not a pretty place, and for me, being enrolled in Law, was a tortured experience which I did not feel connected to nor enjoyed. Fortunately, I was not destined to remain in Hell long: I found myself increasingly enjoying my elective Psychology unit and continued focusing on these studies, eventually finding my way to Paradise, and ultimately being able to work as a Psychologist and eventually a Family Therapist.

Working as a family therapist has given me a wonderful richness of experience to share in clients' lives. For clients to trust me in helping them open up their world has truly been a gift. Clients attend therapy, often feeling helpless, depleted, and incompetent. Yet, by attending psychotherapy and sharing their lives, their hopes and dreams, as well as putting effort into changing their lives, I have had the privilege of witnessing my clients' enormous achievements. This book is a testimony to some of the clients I have seen over the last forty-five years. Their courage and resolve to face incredible difficulties in their lives have been a great inspiration and motivate me to continue in my work.

Psychotherapy: is it science or is it art? This is a vexing question, and I am sure there is no definitive answer. Despite the fact that there are now many training courses which highlight set, standardized processes regarding how to interview clients, and how to work from a particular therapeutic model, I struggle to see psychotherapy as simply a set of techniques and processes that can be manualized and simply followed like a recipe. My belief is that psychotherapy is not just something that the therapist *does*. Psychotherapy is a process between therapist and clients. It is something that involves a *relationship* between the two. It requires trust, honesty, hope, resilience, belief, commitment, and preparation to work together. The process often starts with the therapist being seen by clients to have knowledge and skills; whereas the clients often begin from a position of helplessness, impotence, and failure. However, the process of psychotherapy requires that as time passes, the input from the clients becomes more and more important. The clients' strengths and competence must be acknowledged, encouraged, and integrated in the process of therapy.

This book provides some examples of the fascinating and exciting work I have been honoured to share with a range of clients: individuals, couples and families. The stories also provide some of the seminal experiences I had to help me become a Family Therapist. I also want to offer this work to help remove the mystique from the process of psychotherapy. Yes, it does require a therapist to have formal qualifications and thorough training and experience. That alone, however, will not necessarily result in a therapist doing good psychotherapy. It also requires the therapist to have a good level of self-awareness and an ability to relate to clients on a human level through the process of psychotherapy. It is collaborative work, and the therapist must ensure that the clients have an active involvement in the work. Also, the therapist may provide considerable active input at the beginning of therapy, especially if the clients feel disempowered and impotent. However, it's important that the therapist encourage and enable the clients to believe in themselves and increase their level of competence and self-belief, so that they can own an involvement and recognition in achieving their goals.

All the cases provided in this book were actual clients seen in therapy. Names and other identifying details have been changed or altered to ensure confidentiality. In sharing these cases I extend my thanks and gratitude to these clients who have shared so much of themselves to me. I also thank these clients for teaching me, as well as helping me to develop my skills as a Family Therapist.

The chapters in this book are arranged in such a way as to explore psychotherapy with a range of clients: individuals, couples, and families. While most of my work is with couples and families, the systemic view of psychotherapy that I use as my basic foundation is equally applicable to working with individuals, couples, and families.

Chapter 1 focuses on a family attending family therapy for their fifteen-year-old son's complex symptoms. Although the boy's symptoms are what brings the family to therapy, underlying issues of loss and grief are uncovered in the process, and subsequently dealt with.

Chapter 2 explores the use of paradox in therapy with a young woman who has an eating disorder, and who attended individually, then together with her partner, and also with her family of origin. In using paradox, it was important to understand how she experienced this intervention, and how she made use of the tasks to overcome bulimia and eventually to consolidate her progress. In getting her to record a testimonial video, I wanted the video to be used to help others with similar problems in the future, as well as helping her to shift to the position of "expert" in dealing with bulimia, rather than being a "victim" of the disorder.

Chapter 3 describes psychotherapy using storytelling with a mother and six-year-old daughter, also involving the child's father. The therapy involved the writing of a fairytale to help two parents loosen their stuck and rigid stances which were creating difficulties for their daughter. Although storytelling is often seen as something suitable for children, *at heart, adults are simply grown up little children.*

Chapter 4 recounts the psychotherapy of a psychologist who first attended for supervision and then requested psychotherapy, wanting to focus on her own history to help her manage both professional and relationship issues. In this chapter we are able to see the connection between our professional *self* and our *SELF.*

Chapter 5 outlines the psychotherapy with a woman who had been permanently institutionalized for over 10 years in a psychiatric hospital, and the process of this therapy. Despite the fact that psychotherapy did not appear to be "working", we are able to see what incredible changes can occur when none seemed possible.

Chapter 6 describes short-term, intensive psychotherapy of a fractured, adult family, willing to do what is needed to heal wounds that occurred many decades earlier. It also demonstrates the courage people have in acknowledging their mistakes and personal flaws, and the ensuing benefits this acknowledgement can provide in healing very old wounds.

Chapter 7 recounts two examples of a particular therapeutic intervention, once when it was useful, and then later, when it was simply repeated as a *"technique"*, it proved to be of little value. This experience buoys my view that the mechanical application of a technique or procedure while in some contexts can be effective and helpful, will not automatically have the same value in other contexts.

Chapter 8 tells the story of a family struggling with an adolescent caught between two cultures, and a way of engaging a violent and rigid father to participate in psychotherapy. This offers hope to therapists working with what we sometimes label as *rigid or resistant clients*.

Chapter 9 centres on a young man struck down with anxiety symptoms and intrusive thoughts which were out of his control. Although psychotherapy was useful in helping him start to look at his life, and not just at his symptoms, it also highlights how small, yet extremely significant human experiences during the therapy process can further enhance the reflective process of therapy and consolidate the therapy process. Also, having his wife's participation in therapy was helpful to his improvement.

Finally, Chapter 10 involves a couple who have significant conflict regarding family loyalties and significant difficulties in handling conflicts. Despite each being blaming of the other at first, confronting them to focus on personal change helped them find a way to resolve both the interfamily conflict as well as regaining the ability to love each other and be there more positively for their children.

I hope you enjoy this book.

Acknowledgments

The idea of this book germinated over many years; its gestation period from idea to the written form, however, took about nine months. Being housebound and having to recuperate following a double knee replacement gave me the opportunity to commence the process of documenting the stories that have stayed with me for several decades. These stories have affirmed and sustained my belief in the human spirit and the healing power that we have as human beings.

In writing this book, there are many people who contributed **to my work**, whom I wish to thank. Firstly, my wife, Mary, who has supported me throughout our forty-six years together. Mary's love, care, and patience, especially during my recovery period following surgery, were testimony to her warmth and nurturing nature. I also value Mary's critical feedback and suggestions in reviewing **an** early draft of this book.

My special thanks go to my daughter, Lara, who provided a keen eye on the early draft of this manuscript. Her valuable feedback and helpful suggestions assisted me in preparing the final version of this book. I also wish to thank Anne Holloway, my esteemed colleague of many years, for her input in helping me to finalize the full title of this book. Special mention needs to go to Julie Di Camillo for her photographic skills of the two paintings for the cover of this book. I greatly value her flexibility and technical skills.

My special thanks to my publisher, Mitchell Ginsberg, for his guidance, direction, and critical attention to detail. Mitchell helped me to make the stories in this book come to life. He was so easy to work with and was always available despite being at the other side of the globe.

Finally, I wish to thank my clients who have trusted me with their private and intimate lives, their struggles, and their successes. They are the ones who have helped me to become a Family Therapist. I hope you enjoy the fruits of labour to which all above have contributed.

Aldo Gurgone

Chapter 1
The Rosary

On a warm, summer's day, a new, Italian family entered my therapy room at the recently established Multicultural Psychiatric Centre. I had struggled with the idea of working there, being of Italian origin: I didn't want to be typecast in the role of only working with migrants, but after much thought, I agreed to take a position there. I had been offered the position of Clinical Psychologist at the Centre by the Psychiatrist Superintendent, Dr Boranga, and diplomatically (in my eyes) I initially refused it. After a few days, I re-thought that decision and approached Dr Boranga, to say that I would be willing to take the position for two days per week, so long as I could continue working in my substantive position at a Psychiatric Hospital the other three days. Although I thought that Dr Boranga would be put off by my initial refusal, he was gracious in understanding my situation and offered to assist in supporting this change. Following this, I commenced my work at the Centre, and Dr Boranga referred this Italian family to me. They had contacted him following a radio interview they heard on a multicultural radio program, in which he described how the new Multicultural Psychiatric Centre would operate.

Following the radio program, Giuseppe Giannini, the father in this family, contacted the Centre as he was seriously concerned about his fifteen-year-old son, Marco. After meeting the family, Dr Boranga referred them to me for family therapy.

It was also co-incidental, and fortunate, that a young Psychiatrist who had seen the family in the Emergency Department of a large general hospital, had also given them my name as a Clinical Psychologist who may be able to help them as a family. Although the young Psychiatrist reportedly declined to provide a diagnosis, as the boy was only fifteen years old, in the referral letter, she nonetheless described early signs of psychosis and schizophrenia, as well as an obsessive-compulsive disorder, and an *"overanxious, controlling Italian mother"*. At that stage, I wasn't aware that there was a diagnosis in the DSMIV under the heading of *Overanxious & Controlling Italian Mother!*

While the intake form identified four family members, only three attended the first session. The nineteen-year-old daughter, Rita, was on a teaching practicum at a rural school, and was unable to attend this appointment. However, the mother reassured me that Rita would finish the practicum at the end of that week and would then be able to attend future appointments.

When they entered the therapy room, Elia, the mother, was dressed in black, so my first response to her was to offer her my condolences, and ask her who had died in the family. Immediately she burst into tears and was struggling to speak, and after a minute or two, Giuseppe took over the conversation, saying that his wife had lost three brothers in twenty-two months.

This pattern of Giuseppe speaking whenever his wife was emotionally distressed became evident over time. Otherwise, Giuseppe was a very quiet man, with his wife generally doing most of the talking during sessions. He explained that one of his wife's brothers had died of a heart attack at the age of 49, another brother had died of heat-stroke during an unusually hot summer, and the other brother had died of unknown causes. Giuseppe reported that each death had occurred about 11 months apart. By this stage in the appointment, Elia had gathered herself together and joined the conversation, saying that her brothers had all died in Italy and she hadn't been able to return since the deaths, the last being about three months ago. She described her distress at being so far away and as her mother was elderly, she was fearful and distressed at not being able to return to Italy before her mother died.

This conversation dominated more than half the session, with Elia describing her family, and the fact that she and her husband had been in Australia twenty years. She had not returned to Italy since their arrival in Australia. Elia then explained that both the children were born here, also mentioning that her father died about a year after they came to Australia. Again, she broke into tears and Giuseppe took this cue to again speak on his wife's behalf.

At this point I reflected that I was extremely sad about her many losses, however I understood that they had been referred to me for other reasons, and I would also appreciate understanding these reasons as well. With this, Elia took over the conversation describing their extreme concern about their son Marco who would occasionally break out in "gibberish", which neither she nor Giuseppe could help with or stop. When I asked them to describe what they meant by gibberish, Elia said that he would talk and talk very fast and make sounds, but they couldn't understand what he was saying. It would go on for hours and hours, and no matter what they did, he wouldn't stop.

When I asked them what they did to try to stop him or help him, Elia said she would try to talk to him, to reason with him, sometimes she would make him a camomile drink, at times she would cry, and sometimes even slap him to make him to stop. She said that she didn't know what to do, and didn't understand why it was happening. Elia couldn't identify any reasons for this onset, and it had been going on during the last two or three months. She had taken Marco to the family doctor, who had prescribed a mild tranquilizer, and she had also taken him to the Emergency Department of the general hospital on two separate occasions.

When asking about patterns or possible ideas anyone had about when and why this had started to happen, all three family members couldn't offer anything; they merely reported that it happened exclusively at home, never at school nor in any social situation outside of home. Marco said he didn't know why this was happening. When I asked him to "*show*" me what he did at those times, he baulked, saying that he couldn't do it "*just like that*". Persisting with this line of questioning, I kept asking him to "*show*" it, rather than describe it.

I said I really wanted to understand what was happening, and if he "*showed*" me, it would help me have a better understanding, and thus be better able to assist. With my persistence, Marco initially said it just came on and he couldn't stop it. With further encouragement or insistence from me, he made a tame effort to show me. He simply babbled meaningless sounds that were indecipherable. His parents said that this was a lame attempt by Marco to show what he was like when this babbling started. They said that it was much more intense and he would go on for hours and hours like a racehorse commentator on the radio.

Marco's father then told me that he had taped Marco during one of these occasions, but he had forgotten to bring the audiotape to the session. He would bring it for me to hear at the next session. Elia also said that they had been told about a new Child &

Adolescent Psychiatric Hospital, when they went to the Emergency Department, which might help. However, she and Giuseppe didn't like the idea because they worried about how to explain Marco's absence if visitors came home. They were worried about the stigma of a psychiatric condition. They also explained that they were different to most Italian families, because they had no extended family in Australia. However, they were at their wit's end about what they could do, and they felt helpless.

Before ending the session, I again asked if there was anything else they could tell me, and Giuseppe said it often happened when the phone rang. He was curious to know why this happened with phone calls. In asking how they were informed about the three brother's deaths, Giuseppe said that either Elia's mother or her sister had rung to tell them the terrible news.

At the end of the session, I said that I wasn't sure whether it was a good idea or a bad idea to have Marco admitted to the Child & Adolescent Psychiatric Hospital, and this was important for them as a family to discuss and then decide what was best for Marco. However, if he was hospitalized, I knew the staff there, and would be able to co-ordinate with them. While I didn't want to encourage his parents to see Marco's symptoms as something that was simply a problem inside Marco, I also decided to use Giuseppe's act of taping his son's babbling in a therapeutic way.

I asked Giuseppe to spend an hour with Marco each weekend, with the first half hour getting Marco to "babble" as close as possible to when he did it spontaneously, when he was out of control, and for Giuseppe to tape Marco when he did it. I told Giuseppe that I understood that he was a very caring father and even if this was difficult for him, to nonetheless insist that Marco "do it really well". I explained that it was his job as a father to ensure that Marco did it and for Giuseppe to tape Marco. I also wanted Giuseppe to bring the audio tape he had already made, as well as the new tapes that he would record each weekend. I impressed upon him that the tapes would help me to better understand why this babbling was happening. For the other half hour, I wanted Giuseppe to do something enjoyable with his son. He mentioned that they both enjoyed playing chess, so this could be something they could do together, as well as other pleasant activities as a father and son. The family agreed to attend sessions at the Centre and also to include Rita in future.

At the next session, I spent a little time getting to know Rita and hearing her views on what was happening. Rita quite insightfully recognized the fact that her mother was struggling with Marco's behaviour and she thought that it might be helpful if her mother let Marco alone at those times. Rita also took the opportunity to mention that her mother was very controlling, and treated her as a small child, as she was not allowed to go out alone with friends. Nineteen year old Rita couldn't understand why her mother trusted her to be at university every day on her own, but not to go out at night without a family member. Rita wanted more freedom and while she thought her father would be agreeable to her ideas, her mother insisted on her doing things "properly". Doing things properly meant just doing what her mother wanted; otherwise her mother worried that people they knew would think that Rita was a wayward girl and would think badly of their family.

Elia also mentioned that they had discussed Marco's possible admission to hospital and had decided that they would follow this up in spite of their concerns. Rita had rung the hospital to find out how the admission would work, and was reassured that although Marco would be in hospital during the school week, the staff would drive him to and from school each day, and he could have weekend leave to go home. They told her that during his stay in hospital, Marco would have access to a Psychologist, a Psychiatrist, a Social Worker, and Psychiatric Nurses. During the evenings they also had some group sessions where Marco could participate, and talk about anything that was troubling him.

Although Marco was not happy about this, he agreed to the admission. The family intended to follow this up with the hospital after the session. When I spoke to Giuseppe about the task I had asked him to do, he said it had been difficult. Nonetheless, he had insisted that Marco do the babbling, and he had brought tapes for me to listen to. He also said that they had played chess and was impressed that his son was better than him, despite Giuseppe having prided himself on being the best chess player in his home town. He confessed that they had spent more than half an hour playing chess and he appreciated his son showing that he enjoyed this time together.

The following session revolved around Marco's hospital admission, which I knew about, as the hospital staff had provided me with feedback on his involvement in group activities. Marco was not happy there, and had found it difficult to connect with the other adolescents. He thought that the other patients had serious problems, especially at home, and he really didn't want to be there. He felt he could study better at home, and as he was very academic, he struggled with the fact that many of the other patients in the hospital didn't want to go to school and he felt like a fish out of water.

At this session, I also raised the issue of Elia's losses, and especially the fact that they didn't know the most recent cause of death. With this, Elia broke into tears and Giuseppe took over the conversation, saying that they couldn't find the cause of death and this was of great concern to Elia and the rest of the family, which now consisted of one other brother, a sister and her mother who was in her eighties.

At this juncture I suggested the idea of Elia and Giuseppe, or even the whole family, going to Italy to help Elia grieve. Giuseppe agreed, saying that they had discussed this, and they would do this, sometime in the future. When I questioned why it needed to be in the future, Giuseppe said it was very expensive for all four of them to go, but they could possibly do it once they had paid off their house. When I suggested the possibility of Elia going alone or with Giuseppe, he said that they couldn't leave their children on their own, nor could Elia go on her own as he didn't know how to cook, and he wanted to be there for his wife.

The session ended there, and later I was able to listen to Giuseppe's two tapes. The first tape, which was the original recording that Giuseppe had made, involved Marco making rambling, indecipherable sounds. It was like a chant and reminded me of someone saying the Rosary before a funeral. It was constant verbal rambling, with his mother screaming and crying for him to stop. At times Giuseppe's voice emerged, trying to reason with Marco to do what his mother wanted. Elia sounded very distressed, whilst Marco babbled on relentlessly, and Giuseppe's voice sounded rather helpless.

The second tape involved Giuseppe encouraging Marco to do the babbling and Marco complaining, saying that it was dumb to have to do it. However, after his father insisted, Marco made a poor attempt to babble, but it was slow and interspersed with Giuseppe's insistence. Marco would babble for 20 to 30 seconds and then complain that it was dumb and stupid to do this, and he couldn't understand why he had to do it, as he wanted this to stop.

By the next session Marco had been discharged; the hospital staff had decided that if he was fine and not "babbling" during the two weeks' leave at home, during school holidays, then he could be discharged. The staff apparently didn't think Marco needed to be in hospital as there had not been any recurrence of the babbling either at home or at hospital since his admission. Marco was very happy to be back home, and reported that he hadn't had the urge to do the babbling for quite some time. I asked him to continue practicing the babbling with his father on weekends. When Marco asked why he would need to do the babbling, I explained that if he practiced it under voluntary control, it would help him to stop doing it if it came on by itself. He mused for a while and then said, *"Yeah, I guess that makes sense. But I hate doing it!"*

During this session I again raised the idea of Elia going back to Italy. Once again Elia started crying and saying she couldn't right now, followed by Giuseppe taking over the conversation and while continuing to agree with me that she needed to do it, he put forward all the reasons why it wasn't possible right now! The session ended on this note, and I suggested that at the next session we would ask Dr Boranga to attend to review progress.

Whilst I said that I invited Dr Boranga to the next session to "review progress", what I *wanted* was to get Dr Boranga to support my view about Elia going to Italy to grieve the deaths in her family. Although they referred to me as "Dottore", Dr Boranga was the "Professore", which is a higher status than "Dottore". My intent was to bring in the Cavalry (Dr Boranga) to support my recommendation, so they would do what I wanted. Unfortunately, the farcical session with me outlining to Dr Boranga the work they had done, and my recommendation for Mrs Giannini to go to Italy, didn't go well, despite Dr Boranga's support. When I asked Dr Boranga his opinion about Mrs Giannini going to Italy, he thought for a minute, stroked his chin, and then said, *"Mrs Giannini, Dottore Gurgone is absolutely right and I would strongly recommend that you go to Italy and do the grieving that you need to do."*

Despite Dr Boranga's strong support, I was shocked to see an even more vehement response by both Giuseppe and Elia, diplomatically insisting that it wasn't possible at this stage. Being able to sit back and observe their response to Dr Boranga, allowed me to realize that there was something going on that I didn't understand, so I politely encouraged the end of this interview and asked the family to come to my therapy room.

When everybody was seated, I apologized to Elia and Giuseppe. I said that I realised during the session with Dr Boranga that I hadn't been hearing them, and that I had been pushing them to do something that wasn't right for them. I apologized for this, however I wanted them to help me understand *why* they couldn't go to Italy now. I said I finally heard their message loud and clear in the earlier session. With this Elia burst into tears. After several minutes Giuseppe said, *"She can't go as they may kill her if she goes there."* At first I didn't understand this, and I asked, *"Who would kill your wife, and why would they kill her?"* Giuseppe then paused and looked at his wife and said, *"The mafia! They killed her brother! If she goes there, sooner or later someone in the town will tell her who did it. Then the whole town will go with her to the cemetery and you know what women are like. She'll get very emotional and say to the killer, 'You bastard! Get out of here!' or something like that, and then they are likely to kill her. We can't go back now. We have to wait, until things calm down, and she is able to cope better, and then we will go. We will go as a family. By that stage it will be easier for her. We will go!"*

With this knowledge, I thanked Giuseppe for helping me understand, and I again apologized for trying to push them to do something that they were telling me wasn't right for them. The session ended with getting their feedback on how they felt about the family sessions, and I outlined my views on the progress of therapy thus far. We all agreed that the original reasons for attending therapy had improved and Marco had not had any further episodes of babbling since they started therapy. Rita, who missed several sessions due to study commitments, was vocal. Without being negative about her parents, she wanted to talk about wanting her parents to give both herself and Marco more freedom. She especially wanted more freedom to go out with friends without having a chaperone. Nonetheless, she did acknowledge that over the course of the family therapy sessions, her parents had started to be less controlling, which Rita wanted to continue.

I also suggested that as I would soon be away at a Family Therapy Conference, we could start to space sessions further apart—it had been fortnightly until then—that I would see them in a month and then review progress. At the family therapy conference, I was fortunate to attend a presentation on the importance of Culture in Family Therapy conducted by Nada Miocevic, a wonderful family therapist working in Melbourne. I was so impressed with her work that I talked to her about this family, and through this discussion I was able to broaden my thinking to other ways for the family to grieve the loss of these family members.

On my return from the Conference, I saw the family and we reviewed how they were going as a family. They reported that they were fine. There hadn't been any recurrence of the babbling, everyone felt better as a family; Rita was happier with more freedom, being allowed to go to parties with her university friends; both Giuseppe and Elia said that despite their concerns about what their 'paesani' might say if they knew that they were allowing their daughter to go out without a family member present, they trusted Rita to do the right thing. Also, Marco was doing well at school and asked about what he would need to do if he wanted to become a psychologist, although his preference was still medicine.

At the end of the session, I suggested that we meet in a month's time, however, I requested that the session be at their house, which was relatively close to the Centre. I also wanted the session to be at a time that all four members of the family were present, so I would accommodate their preferred date and time, even if it needed to be in the evening. For this forthcoming session, I asked Elia to provide a photo of each of her brothers, explaining that she needed to be prepared to relinquish the photos. I also asked Giuseppe to buy three candles, and three plants from a nursery—beautiful plants that he and his wife both loved, for our next appointment. Finally, I asked them to choose a place where they may plant them, and to have a spade ready for this event. As we were about to end the session, Marco, wide-eyed, said, *"I know what you are going to do!"* I replied, *"What am I going to do?"* and he said, *"You're going to do a séance!"* I replied,

"Hey Marco, that sounds like an interesting idea. Maybe we can check it out when we meet again."

I arrived at their house in the early dark of evening, for the session. On answering the doorbell, they showed me into the kitchen which had a dining table and chairs, and we caught up with what had happened for them since their last appointment. After the social niceties, I asked Giuseppe and Elia whether they had the various things and implements that I had asked them to prepare. Giuseppe said that he had everything ready and that they had prepared four holes, four candles, and four rose bushes. He explained they also wanted to include Elia's father in this ritual, because they hadn't been able to go back to Italy after he died.

Giuseppe said that he had decided to perform the ritual on the side of the house, in order to have greater privacy. As both the front garden and the back garden were more exposed to the neighbours, they wanted to do this ritual privately. They had already dug the holes for each family member, and Marco, being a strong fifteen-year-old boy, had taken responsibility for digging the holes. I accompanied the four family members to the side of the house using the four lit candles to provide the light. They had prepared the photos, and I asked Elia to say a few words at each hole, to symbolize who was being laid to rest. With due respect for the occasion, she started with her father, and told him how precious he was to her, how she missed him, and how she regretted not being there at the end of his life. It was very emotional, yet she was able to express her tears whilst still saying what was important for her to say. She then kissed the photo and placed it in the hole, then Marco poured some soil over the photo, before Rita planted the rose in the hole. Marco then poured more soil over the exposed roots of the rose bush, to ensure the rose was well grounded. One by one, Elia took each of the other photos, spoke to each brother, kissed the photo, and then placed it in the hole. Finally, her daughter and son did their part in this important ritual in laying each family member to rest. Giuseppe then had a hose ready to water the plants and ensure that any air bubbles in the root system were removed. Once this was done, Elia placed a lit candle under each rose bush.

After performing this ritual, the family asked me to join them for coffee and biscuits in their kitchen. We spent time drinking coffee, eating the biscuits that Elia had baked that day, and hearing stories from Elia and Giuseppe about the various family members that had died.

Giuseppe and Elia also advised me that as Marco was in Year 10, they had decided that they would all return to Italy for closure when he finished high school after Year 12. As I was about to leave, they gave me some of the biscuits and fresh eggs from their chickens. I thanked them, and they expressed their gratitude that I conducted the session in their home. They also offered thanks to my wife for being very accommodating, as I would be getting home so late.

The next session took place towards the end of the year, just before Christmas, and at this appointment, despite my colour blindness, I noticed that Elia was wearing a navy blue dress. When I commented on this, Elia appeared rather sheepish, saying that Rita and Marco had insisted that she could now wear colours. She only acceded to their insistence, agreeing to wear dark colours as it was now a year since the last loss. Elia explained that in her region of Italy, after a year of mourning, it was acceptable for women to start wearing colours again. The session was otherwise uneventful, as everything was going well. Rita had done well at university and had another year before she qualified as a high school teacher. Marco performed well at school and was in the top classes that would make it possible to eventually get into the university courses he was considering. Giuseppe and Elia both seemed proud of their children. As they were about to leave the therapy room, Giuseppe said, *"Oh by the way, we have a little problem, and maybe you can help us. The newspaper man who delivers the morning newspaper, threw a paper on Saturday, and it broke one of the main branches of a rose bush. What should we do?"* Before I could answer, Marco chimed in and said, *"Don't worry dad. The rose bush is still okay as there are still several branches which are strong!"* All I could say was, *"There you go Giuseppe, you have a very smart son who understands many things."* The session ended there with the proviso that if they needed to come back to see me, they knew how to contact me.

In this story, there were several noteworthy aspects. Firstly, my having recognized the cultural significance of Elia wearing black. This was a critical issue, allowing me to connect Marco's symptoms with the losses suffered by this family. Secondly, the use of paradox, when I asked Marco to "show me" what he did. Although I sometimes use paradox in my therapy, I am mindful to ensure that it is not experienced by clients as demeaning or hurtful, wherever possible. Through paradox I was able to help Marco gain control of his symptoms; by asking him to *play* with them by voluntarily producing the babbling sounds which he believed he couldn't produce, in spite of the fact that he couldn't stop the babbling when it occurred involuntarily. Although we never really *addressed* the symptoms apart from asking Marco to produce them voluntarily, the symptoms never resurfaced again throughout many months of therapy. Thirdly, while my well-intentioned suggestion that returning to Italy would help the grieving process was theoretically sound, in their wisdom, the family knew that this was neither possible nor helpful. In their own way, they tried to tell me that it wasn't right for them.

Sometimes it is difficult to appreciate that your ideas are not necessarily the best. Fortunately, however, I eventually understood that my intervention was creating *resistance* in the family. When I realized this, I had the good sense to apologize, and then the family helped me to explore a creative way of being able to assist them. Steve de Shazer (who developed Solution Focused Brief Therapy) said that when clients are being "resistant", it means that the therapist is *doing something TO the client, and not something WITH the client.*

Finally, while the family did not attend because of cultural difficulties between the two generations, the parents were eventually able to relax their rigid ideas about social freedom for their young adult daughter, after first focusing on the presenting symptoms and the grief. This change was a bonus. The family's healing power was quite evident. I learnt much from this family.

I also want to express my special thanks to Nada Miocevic for her contribution to helping me think through a creative way of providing this family with the assistance they needed, in a way that was appropriate for them.

Chapter 2
Caitlin: A Comma Not a Full Stop!

I had been working in a psychiatric hospital for about a year. Initially, I only agreed to take this position because I was told that after that year I would be able to reduce to part-time so I could also establish my private practice. Nonetheless, I thoroughly enjoyed my work at the hospital. At that time, I only had five or six years' experience working with patients with mental health issues. Through my experience at the hospital, I developed good relationships with staff from all the different disciplines: psychiatry, social work, nursing, occupational therapy, as well as my clinical psychologist colleagues.

One day the psychiatrist superintendent asked me to see a young woman who was not an in-patient in the hospital. He was seeing her at a nearby Mental Health Out-Patient Clinic. She was referred to him for bulimia. After assessing her, he felt his medications would be of little use, but he believed that psychotherapy would be helpful. Although I wasn't assigned to that clinic, he offered to approve my seeing her as an out-patient at the hospital, explaining that she had already agreed to this.

We arranged to meet. She came to the psychiatric hospital and although she was extremely nervous at being seen there, the first session went well. She was able to describe the difficulties she had with food and her history around these difficulties. At that time, in the early 1980s, while there was a burgeoning literature about anorexia nervosa, there was very little written about bulimia. I was only able to source a few medical articles on the subject, and they suggested a very poor prognosis for sufferers.

Caitlin, in her very early twenties, was an attractive woman and despite believing that she was "fat", appeared only slightly overweight. She told me that she had no difficulties with food growing up and had only became conscious of her weight when she went on an exchange program to the United States, around the age of fifteen to sixteen. Despite enjoying the beginning of the exchange program, Caitlin began feeling a sense of competition from Gloria, the host family's daughter, who returned prematurely from her exchange in Australia. Caitlin said that she felt welcomed by Gloria's mother while Gloria was in Australia on exchange, but that she felt that her relationship with Gloria's mother deteriorated after Gloria returned home and the friends she had developed at Gloria's school started to treat her differently; Caitlin felt ostracized. She became unhappy and homesick. Having been raised in a family where one finished the things they started, Caitlin felt she had no option but to remain on the exchange program until its planned completion. She became increasingly withdrawn and depressed, and gradually started to eat more and more. Caitlin found it hard to enjoy the last few months of the exchange.

Caitlin began feeling self-conscious about her weight when she returned home and her older brother teased her about having gained weight while she was away. Nevertheless, she found it hard to resist eating many of the things that she had grown to enjoy as comfort foods whilst in the US. After Caitlin's school friends also commented on her weight, she became extremely self-conscious and eventually learned to purge, by touching the back of her tongue and throat with a finger. Caitlin eventually became able to purge at will, even without touching the back of her tongue or throat.

Her friends noticed that she was getting slimmer, which encouraged Caitlin to keep purging. However, while she had been living out of home and doing a degree in Fine Arts during the last two years, the over-eating and purging had gotten out of control. About a year earlier Caitlin sought a psychiatric assessment and was referred to a trainee clinical psychologist who helped her reduce the purging, using behaviour therapy. She found this helpful, and stopped treatment when the trainee's placement ended. However, after a few months Caitlin reverted back to over-eating and purging.

At the time we met, Caitlin was doing this more frequently than ever before. I asked why she chose to get treatment *now* and not previously, nor conversely, in a few months' time. Caitlin said that she had recently moved in with her boyfriend, and she was struggling to keep this secret from him. She believed that if he found out, he would "dump" her. Her bingeing and purging were worse now than they had ever been.

At the end of the session, I agreed to see Caitlin weekly, to help her achieve her goals of being able to eat normally and not overeat, nor purge. Caitlin appreciated hearing that I believed she could make significant changes, especially given that she had already made changes with the previous psychologist. I explained to her that since she had gained control of her eating and purging before, I was confident that she could achieve it again. I also asked Caitlin how she felt about seeing me in a psychiatric hospital setting, and she admitted her fears about having serious problems and being put into a *"madhouse"*. Caitlin needed reassurance that she was not mad and that I was only seeing her at the hospital because they did not have a therapy room available at the Clinic.

We agreed to therapy for a period of six months with a review, at which point we would decide how to proceed. As Caitlin was familiar with keeping a diary of her eating and bingeing from her previous therapy, I asked her to continue recording them, but that I also wanted her to do something different. When she had a bout of eating and purging, *I wanted her to purge again, an hour later. Also, if she hadn't purged at all that day, then, at the end of the day, I wanted her to purge.* I asked her to record these events and to bring them to each session. I also told Caitlin that I wanted to know if she understood what I was asking her to do, and whether she needed me to explain the rationale for this. She said that she understood exactly why I was asking her to do this and she was fine with it.

Caitlin committed to this therapy, and attended sessions weekly. From the beginning, I encouraged her to raise with me in session if there was anything that I was asking her to do that she had trouble with, or didn't understand. This was especially important as I was using a paradoxical approach (by asking her to purge an hour after purging, or by the end of the day if she hadn't purged that day). I wanted to be sure that Caitlin had a positive understanding of the tasks and didn't interpret them as punitive ordeals. I repeatedly encouraged Caitlin to ask me questions about my interventions; she consistently insisted that she both understood and didn't have any problem with what I asked of her.

Although I was initially seeing Caitlin individually, I asked her to bring her family of origin to some sessions. Caitlin's father was of Italian extraction, and her mother was Australian, of English and Irish background. I explained that family sessions would allow her to disclose what she was going through, and to get support from them if things became more difficult in her life.

Caitlin said that although she never discussed these things with her family, she felt quite supported by them and agreed to invite them to a session. However, she reiterated that her biggest fear was that her boyfriend might find out and then reject her.

Although Caitlin said that she would contact her family from the first time we discussed family therapy, she repeatedly presented numerous reasons preventing her from seeing or calling them to invite them to attend. Eventually, six weeks after Caitlin commenced therapy, her family attended the first of three sessions. When they arrived for their first session together, all three — father, mother and older brother — initially appeared quite cautious and uncomfortable, as they were unsure about why they had been asked to attend. My interpretation of their guardedness was that they expected to be blamed for Caitlin's problems.

As the session progressed, however, all three seemed relieved that I wanted them to help me understand anything they could come up with that may have related to Caitlin's problems. Gradually, they became more open about their family, including demonstrating their sincere concern for Caitlin. Towards the end of the session, they expressed a strong desire to be there for Caitlin. Even her brother opened up, apologizing for the times he had made fun of her about her being "fat". Caitlin later expressed how much she appreciated this spontaneous apology, as she had never mentioned to her brother how she felt shame and embarrassment at his comments about her weight. Therefore, receiving an unsolicited apology from him felt genuine and real. Her brother told her that he would be there for her in any way she needed, and from that session, they started spending more time together.

Her parents were open and supportive of Caitlin. They were surprised at the difficulties that Caitlin had experienced in the US and they felt bad that she had not been able to talk to them about what she had experienced. They reassured her that while she had moved out, she always had a place in their home. They wanted to support her in whatever way they could. They also wanted some guidance from me so that they could understand all this "bulimia stuff". We discussed what bulimia was and I supported Caitlin in describing the disorder, as she was the one *living* it. She was able to open up to them in ways that had previously seemed impossible for her. At the end of the session, Caitlin's family appeared very supportive and interested in being there for her on her journey to overcome bulimia. They were happy to attend whenever they were required. Through the other sessions that they attended, the family demonstrated ongoing support and love towards Caitlin. I believe this was of great benefit to Caitlin, as she was able to fully recognize that her family was there for her. In my opinion this also helped her take the ultimate risk to trust her boyfriend with this secret.

Caitlin started going out with with her boyfriend, Lincoln, some 4-5 months before she commenced therapy with me. They had dated and after a few months, as both were due to renew their respective leases, they discussed moving in together and finally decided to do this. Caitlin moved from a shared house into Lincoln's apartment, as this was more comfortable. While she was excited to think that someone as mature, intelligent, and romantic as Lincoln was really interested in her, Caitlin was also experiencing huge anxiety, due to both her low self-esteem, and her binge-purging having once again become out of control. I assumed that this anxiety exacerbated Caitlin's eating behaviour, since she did not believe that Lincoln would stay with her if he knew what she was really like.

During the early sessions, when we discussed her family attending, I also suggested the possibility of inviting Lincoln. I noticed how Caitlin avoided dealing with this suggestion and I did not persist with this at the time, leaving that issue for later, when our therapeutic relationship was stronger. However, Caitlin kept raising her fear of the consequences of Lincoln finding out about her binge-purging. This gave me the opportunity to bring it to the forefront of therapy. Over two sessions, we explored possible outcomes of Caitlin's eventual disclosure of her eating problem to Lincoln. Doing two-chair work, with Caitlin playing the part of herself and then the part of Lincoln, helped her take the plunge and disclose this "dark" side of her personality. After the first of these sessions, Caitlin went home and plucked up the courage to tell Lincoln directly and explicitly about this secret side of her (as she believed, incorrectly, that he already had some vague sense of her purging). She was staggered at his response to her disclosure, when he said that he was prepared to attend therapy sessions with her. She couldn't believe that he could accept her after learning what she was really like.

Although Lincoln had offered to attend therapy sessions after her disclosure, Caitlin elected to have one more session on her own before he came along to therapy. I assumed at the time that Caitlin still didn't trust that Lincoln would accept her, and expected that he would eventually reject her if she gave him more time to think about it. Nevertheless, Lincoln attended the following session together with Caitlin. He seemed a quiet and mature young man about five years older than Caitlin. Lincoln was in his final year of Social Work study, a course he had settled on after attempting several others and ultimately realizing that he did not want to become a wealthy entrepreneur. He said that he wanted to work in an area primarily aligned with his social conscience and that from the beginning, the Social Work course felt like *"home"*.

The first session went well, and Lincoln expressed a deep love for Caitlin. He wanted to share a life with her and was prepared to do whatever he could to support her through this, as well as through any other struggles she and he may have in the future. I sensed that Caitlin was unquestionably amazed by this, while at the same time she found it difficult to believe. At the end of that session, we agreed to continue therapy, with the understanding that all three of us would have a say in who would attend the sessions from session to session. Over the next few months, Lincoln attended about half the sessions, and also once with Caitlin's family. By that session, Caitlin and Lincoln had talked about getting engaged, and had set a tentative date for the end of the year, by which time they would have completed their degrees.

Caitlin was making good progress with her bulimia symptoms. She reported significant improvement within a few sessions of undertaking the task of purging an hour after first purging, or at the end of the day if she hadn't purged that day. At the beginning of therapy, Caitlin said that she was bingeing and purging up to seven times a day, however within three weeks, this reduced to about once a day, and after three months, it was happening only once or twice per week. Although Caitlin made good progress by the end of the six-month timeframe, she said she wanted to continue with further sessions, as she was gaining a lot, not only with her eating problem, but also with her level of self-esteem and her relationship with Lincoln.

During a period where she attended on her own for a few sessions, Caitlin described a dream she had experienced. In her dream there was a young woman in an art gallery who was looking at all the art on the walls. There was also a stranger there, who rather than looking at the art on the wall was looking at, and studying, the young woman. While we did explore the dream somewhat, Caitlin didn't appear to benefit much from our exploration. However, a few days later, while I was out to lunch, Caitlin popped by my office and left me one of her paintings. When I opened the wrapping and saw her name on the painting (see Figure 1), I realized that it was a painting of her dream.

We spent most of the next session focussing on the painting and what it meant to her. Eventually, Caitlin interpreted that *she* was the woman in the dream. However, the image of the woman was a tall, pencil-line image and quite different to her body shape. The "**stranger**" (her word) who was looking at her could only be seen from behind, so there weren't any recognizable features to identify him. In exploring the dream and the painting, Caitlin eventually decided that if the stranger was anyone, it was me the therapist. We then spent considerable time exploring what this meant in the process of therapy.

FIGURE 1: Painting of dream of woman at Art Gallery

What did this mean to Caitlin? Was she still feeling under scrutiny in spite of the fact that we had developed a sound therapeutic relationship? Did she feel I didn't trust her? Did she not trust me? All these and other questions were explored as we analysed the dream painting. It was also interesting to explore the shapes and colours used in the painting. The woman was tall and thin. Her image was faint and almost transparent; quite different to Caitlin's actual shape and presence. Although there was some colour in the art on the wall, the rest of the painting was dark and drab, with little life or vitality. Caitlin acknowledged that the energy in both the form and the colours of the painting were mute and sombre.

By Spring that year, Caitlin was progressing well, reporting consistent improvement. She felt in control of her eating and she said that she did not feel compelled to purge. Caitlin was also very positive about her life and her relationship with Lincoln. After the first six sessions Caitlin attended fortnightly, and at the six-monthly review, we agreed to have monthly reviews, since both Caitlin and Lincoln were getting close to their final exams and assessments. As she was progressing well, I also asked Caitlin if she would participate in a videotaped interview once her exams and assessments were over, where she could describe her experience of therapy. This was particularly important for me, as I was using a paradoxical approach. I wanted as much feedback as possible from Caitlin to clarify what her experience was like in being asked to actively perform some of the symptoms (purging) she had come to therapy to *stop doing*. She said she would be happy to record an interview, and we discussed possible dates.

As I was also a part-time lecturer in the Psychology Department at the same university that Caitlin attended, I contacted the Audio-Visual Unit there, to see if we could arrange a video recording. The only date available was a few days before Christmas, and fortuitously, that was convenient for both of us. At the appointed time and date, I asked Caitlin to advise me how she wanted to shoot the interview; whether she wanted to be seen on camera or not; whether she wanted her name or a pseudonym used; and various other preferences she had, while the audio-visual equipment was being set up.

Caitlin preferred to use the name Natasha and not to be seen on camera, so the interview was shot from behind, with my face in view. Prior to the interview, I provided Caitlin with a list of possible questions to ensure that nothing greatly surprising would occur for her at the last minute. I also explained to Caitlin that by suggesting this interview, I was asking her a favour. I wanted her honest feedback on her experience of therapy. In due course, if she approved of me using this videotape, I might be able to use it either with other people who were going through something similar to what she had gone through; or for training colleagues who would be working with clients experiencing the same problems. Apart from the videotape being a useful tool for me professionally, I wanted to use this process as a way of affirming and consolidating Caitlin's incredible progress, and to minimize any regression.

The interview went well, and we covered most of the planned areas. Although most of the feedback Caitlin provided was replicating what she had said in the previous therapy sessions, there were a few things that she said on camera which surprised me. One of my biggest concerns when working paradoxically was remaining aware of *how* the client experienced the paradoxical task. It would be problematic if the client experienced the paradox as an ordeal or as punishment. It was imperative that the client could rationalize and experience the paradoxical task as a helpful and therapeutic experience.

One of the surprising and valuable things that Caitlin said in the interview was, *"Although I understood the reason why I should purge an hour after I had binged and already purged, I couldn't understand why I needed to purge when I had a good day. I felt that I had worked so hard with my little heart to not binge, that it wasn't fair that I had to then purge, after being such a good little girl!"*

Obviously, the purpose of getting Caitlin to purge a second time, an hour later, was for her to experience purging as a very *"unpleasant sensation"*. The way she had been purging was to throw up immediately on eating a box of biscuits, or an entire cake. Immediately after eating, she would induce vomiting, which was only mildly unpleasant. However, by inducing the vomiting a considerable time after bingeing and purging (an hour after eating and vomiting), she would be vomiting juices in her stomach which would be extremely unpleasant, and with a lingering after-taste. Worse still, at the end of the day, when she had no fresh food in her stomach and only gastric juices, inducing vomiting would be an extremely unpleasant experience that would discourage her from purging in the long term. Therefore, it was interesting that on the one hand Caitlin could understand the reasoning for purging again after an hour, yet on the other hand she didn't understand and appreciate having to purge at the end of a day when she had been *"such a good little girl"*. Nevertheless, she appeared to trust me sufficiently to perform the task, despite not fully understanding my rationale.

The video needed to be edited, and due to the University's Christmas/Summer break, this took several months. In April, on a chilly evening, I met with Caitlin and Lincoln to review the footage. I wanted Lincoln there as well, in order to provide Caitlin with feedback and support, to help her decide if I could use the video. By the time we started viewing the video, night had fallen, and we huddled together in a big, empty, and cold theatre, the only place in the hospital with the capacity for playing the video. Watching, I remember being moved by the genuineness of Caitlin's advice to potential sufferers of bulimia who might see this video in the future. She was encouraging, saying not to give up hope and to maintain self-belief. Caitlin was inspirational in encouraging others to seek help, to involve family members, to get their support, and generally to never give up.

It was cold and dark in the theatre, and towards the end of the video I heard some muffled sounds. When the video ended, I realised that Caitlin had been crying. I found some tissues, handed them to her and asked what her tears were saying. She paused, and said, *"It's a comma, not a full stop!"* This statement was extremely meaningful to me. After a long silence, Caitlin explained that while she *did* feel that she had made progress, she still continued to deal with an internal struggle. Caitlin said she felt comfortable about what she had said on the video, although she still had to work hard at times. Before they left, I asked them to take time to discuss their ideas about giving me permission to use the videotape.

I waited a few months to hear back from Caitlin. She and Lincoln had become engaged after completing their studies and I knew that each of them had applied for graduate positions. I received several telephone messages from Caitlin advising me that she was still going well and that they both consented to my using the video as I saw fit. She also advised me that Lincoln had gotten a job, and about a month later, Caitlin also got a job teaching art at a school, which she wanted before trying to make a living as an artist.

About two months later I received an unmarked package via the hospital's reception. I asked who it was from, however, no name had been left by the person. When I opened the package, I discovered a small oil painting of a naked woman (see Figure 2) with her arms outstretched, appearing to regale in the enjoyment of life. The woman was open in every way and full of life. The colours were vibrant, bright, and lively. It was signed by Caitlin. This was such a refreshing painting, and I took it to mean that this was the self-portrait of her now, as compared to the Caitlin depicted in her dream, who in the earlier drawing was being diagnosed and studied. I believe I understood her comment, *"It's a comma, not a full stop!"* I trusted her to live her life together with the struggle she had at times, knowing that she had the courage and resilience to deal with what came in life.

FIGURE 2: Self Portrait

Although I never saw Caitlin again, I believe she kept in touch with me by referring two separate cousins for therapy at different stages of her life. This helped assuage my curiosity, as it gave me, in both cases, an opportunity to find out that Caitlin and Lincoln had married and about three years later Caitlin was still teaching art at school, and eager to expand her career.

I learned a great deal from working with Caitlin, her family, and Lincoln, which has helped me over many years. The use of paradoxical and other interventions can be useful, as well as harmful, and I have continued to check with my clients on how they experience what I ask them to do. Caitlin's feedback on the video was extremely helpful to me in my development, to my trainees, as well as to many clients who had similar issues to Caitlin's.

Despite her fears, Caitlin's eventual agreement to invite her family, and subsequently to involve Lincoln in her therapy demonstrated a huge level of trust in me, as well as the incredible value of including the family and other relationships in an individual's therapy. The family provided a wonderful support for Caitlin. Lincoln's involvement in the therapy sessions was also truly valuable. While not all families and partners may be as supportive as Caitlin's, over the years I have found that many families and partners, when invited to attend therapy sessions with a loved one going through a difficult time, provide a wonderful resource to the therapy process.

Chapter 3
Once Upon a Time

Cynthia, a beautiful woman in her early thirties, and her six-year-old daughter Lexie, were referred to me by Lois Achimovich, a child psychiatrist, and one of the most influential supervisors in my development as a family therapist. When Cynthia arrived together with Lexie, she said that she wanted help with her daughter. Cynthia explained that over the last few months Lexie had changed from a happy little girl to being sad most of the time, and being particularly unhappy when going to school and to bed. Cynthia was very much a "New Age" person who wanted help for her daughter, but didn't want Lexie to end up on medication.

In providing a developmental history, Cynthia explained that while Lexie's conception was unplanned, when she and Lewis, Lexie's father, discovered that Cynthia was pregnant, they were nonetheless equally happy about having a baby. They enjoyed the pregnancy, which was uneventful. They had a successful home-birth. They were both Sannyasins, or Orange People, a term used for followers of the Indian Guru Osho Bhagwan. Cynthia and Lewis separated when Lexie was about three years old, after some couple-therapy sessions they had undertaken for communication problems.

The separation was amicable and for quite some time both Cynthia and Lewis provided a good secure base for Lexie as she moved between homes, although this had changed in the last few months. Lewis started a new relationship with Lucy, another Sannyasin, soon after separating from Cynthia. The three of them knew one another through their association with the Orange People, and got on very well. About two years ago, when Lexie was about four years old, Lucy became pregnant, and gradually, Lewis asked to spend less time with Lexie. This issue didn't phase Cynthia, and at first it seemed that Lexie wasn't greatly affected by the reduced contact with her father. However, after Lucy gave birth to Ryan, Lewis further reduced the contact time with Lexie.

Until that time, all parenting arrangements had been made directly between Cynthia and Lewis, without the need for lawyers or the Family Law Court. However, a few months after Ryan's birth, Cynthia, who had no need to undertake Assertion Training, confronted Lewis with the fact that she thought that he was losing touch with his daughter, and that he needed to "have balls" and take responsibility as a father. She impressed upon him that he had *two* children, and although he now had a son, he still had a daughter, who also needed him to be available!

Apparently, Lewis did not take this well and began having even less contact with both Cynthia and Lexie. The situation deteriorated further when one evening, Cynthia arrived at Lewis and Lucy's home unannounced and drunk, criticizing them both and saying that if Lewis wasn't man enough to take his fathering seriously, she might move to spare Lexie exposure to an emotionally unavailable father. Again, instead of opening up the communication between them, this only served to further alienate Lewis and Lucy.

Several months passed, and one day, to Cynthia's surprise, Lewis asked to meet. It seemed that he and Lucy had discussed the issue of Lexie's paternity, and Lewis wasn't sure whether he was in fact Lexie's birth father. Cynthia was dumbstruck and enraged that Lewis would even think this, let alone raise it with her. After regaining her composure from the shock of Lewis' disclosure, Cynthia scoffed at the suggestion, even though Lewis reminded her that they had an "open relationship" around the time of Lexie's conception, and that they both had multiple sexual partners within their Sannyasin community also during that time. Lewis left the meeting saying that he would stop making child support payments for Lexie, until Cynthia submitted to a DNA examination to confirm that Lexie was definitely his biological child.

Cynthia ruefully told Lewis what he could do with his DNA test, and that she wanted no further contact with either him or his partner. Following this meeting, Lexie's behaviour deteriorated to the point that Cynthia sought therapy for her. Whilst it was difficult to ascertain to what extent Lexie was exposed to this saga, it seemed clear that the ongoing conflict between her parents was definitely connected with Lexie's mood changes and her ability to feel secure, both at home and school.

At the initial interview with Cynthia, *"dickhead"* was the least colourful descriptor she used for Lewis. He was a *"low-life ... a piece of shit ... a scumbag ..."* and many other things which I chose not to remember. When I suggested that it might be useful to invite Lewis to a future appointment, Cynthia was ambivalent. She could see that having a neutral person in the room could help to keep them both focused on Lexie's needs, but at the same time, Cynthia stated that she had lost respect for Lewis as he progressively relinquished his role as father to Lexie.

At the end of the session I agreed to work with Cynthia and Lexie, also suggesting that Cynthia contact Lewis to see if he would be prepared to attend a session either on his own, or together with Cynthia. Cynthia agreed to let Lewis know and further appointments were made. Between the first and the second appointment, I decided to write a story attempting to assist Cynthia to view Lewis' actions in a different light, to become more aware of her own beliefs and less reactive to Lewis and therefore reducing the conflict. This was the story that emerged:

Once upon a time in a far-off land, a beautiful young princess was travelling through her kingdom. Through her travels, all the handsome and wealthy young men sought to court her, hoping that they could convince her to marry. However, the princess said that she was not yet ready to marry and that when the right time arrived, she would know. She enjoyed meeting her subjects and learning of the many things people did in her kingdom. She was happy and kind, and her people loved her and opened their houses and their hearts to her. One day, she noticed a stranger who was different to her people, and she asked one of her subjects who this stranger was. She was told that the stranger was a prince from another kingdom to the East. She was also told that he was strong and brave and that one day he would become king of his land.

The princess was so taken by the stranger, that she asked one of her servants to invite him to a feast being held in her honour. When the stranger accepted the invitation, the princess invited him to sit next to her, so she could ask him about his kingdom and the customs of his people. During the feast, the princess grew more and more attracted to the stranger, who was handsome and strong. As he spoke about his land and his people, the princess was able to notice that the way he talked about them showed a deep love and affection towards them. This further attracted the princess to the stranger. After this meeting, they parted; however, the princess could not get the stranger out of her mind. The more time passed, the more her thoughts revolved around the stranger and what a wonderful man he appeared to be.

   The princess then asked her servant to invite the stranger to go horse-riding with her. The stranger accepted the offer and they spent the afternoon riding and enjoying each other's company, not noticing where they were riding. At nightfall, they noticed that they were far from where they had commenced their ride, and unsure about how to return in the dark. However, as they were near a small town, they asked someone from the town if there was an inn where they could spend the night. They were told there was a very good inn in the town and they were shown to it. Indeed, the innkeeper was a jolly man who was friendly and full of laughter. He arranged a banquet for the two, and had the best room at the inn prepared for them. They ate and drank to their hearts' content and had a wonderful night to remember. In fact, they enjoyed themselves so much that night that they both realized that they had drunk too much wine and needed to sleep. As they sought leave from the innkeeper they noticed an old hag at the corner of the inn selling all manner of potions and salves. Being drawn to the old hag, they noticed that she had many potions. However, the one potion that caught their eye was one that was labeled: "To Make Beautiful Children".

   When they saw this, immediately they looked at each other with surprise, and in unison, both said, "No! Is that possible?" So, they asked the old hag if it was true that the potion helped to make beautiful children. She assured them that it was true and that they could have a bottle. The princess and the stranger looked at each other in delight; however, the stranger's face turned to sadness when he told the old hag that he had no money with him, so he would need to return the next day in order to pay for the bottle. The hag stroked her chin and said that they did not have to pay the next day, but to prove that the potion worked, the stranger would have to make payment a year and a day after the birth of the child. With this, the stranger and the princess took the potion and quickly went to their bedroom.

   Both were tired, yet were in good spirits from the day's events, and they embraced as two lovers who had found each other. Their embrace ignited a passion within, and the princess then remembered about the potion that the old hag had given them. The stranger then took the potion and, emptying its contents into a silver goblet, passed the potion to the princess. Taking the goblet to her sweet, rosy lips, the princess drank the potion to the last drop, whereupon she turned to her partner and they joined in the most sensual of embraces. There the two lovers spent the night in a deep loving embrace.

Upon waking, the lovers dressed and enjoyed a sumptuous breakfast. With their horses fed and watered, they were able to gallop away and return to where their servants waited for them. On their ride back, they looked at each other in such a way that others understood that a magical encounter had occurred between them the previous night. The princess realized that she had found the man of her dreams, and the stranger, whose name was Prince Aron, also knew that a union had been formed, which mortals could not undo. On arriving at their base, Aron asked his princess to visit his father's kingdom, to meet the king and queen and other family. The princess was happy to go to Aron's kingdom, however she explained that her love for her father and mother was such that she first needed to go to them and seek their blessings. With this understanding, they prepared to travel for two days to attend her parents' royal palace.

As they entered the palace gates, the royal subjects cheered and smiled to see the beautiful young princess together with her handsome partner. The king and queen were relieved at the return of their daughter. When the princess told them of her deep love for Aron and their desire to go to his father's kingdom with the ultimate intention of marriage, they somehow understood that something special had happened, and despite the suddenness of this decision, they gave their blessings to both their daughter and to her chosen prince.

Several days later, they set off for Aron's kingdom. Although it took a few days to arrive, the kingdom was already abuzz with news about the imminent arrival of Prince Aron and the beautiful princess he had found. When they entered the city gates, there was cheering and rejoicing. The king and queen were enamoured with the princess, and they could not have been happier when they learned that the couple had decided to marry. Although they spoke to both their son and his future queen about the importance of marriage, and that they needed to ensure that it wasn't based on a whim. The king and queen were pleasantly assured by both how much in love Aron and the princess were, and the depth of the young couple's commitment.

When it was announced that Prince Aron was to marry, all the subjects rejoiced in delight. Arrangement were quickly made, and the princess's family travelled to Prince Aron's land for the wedding. The wedding was magical, with nothing spared to ensure that this day would be remembered forever more. The princess wore the most beautiful wedding gown and the Prince was at his most handsome best. The subjects cheered and rejoiced at this wonderful event, and the parents were delighted to see their child choose a partner for life, certain that they could not have chosen better themselves.

Time passed, and everyone in the kingdom became aware that the princess was soon to bear a child. This was the best news that they could wish for. They rejoiced in planning for the birth of the royal baby. When the time came for the princess to give birth, the King declared a national holiday to celebrate the birth of a beautiful princess named Anna. Her skin was soft as silk, and the colour of milk. Her hair was golden and every feature of her face reminded everyone of the beauty of her parents. Anna was a healthy child, loved by all who saw her. Whenever anyone mentioned anything about Anna's beauty, both her parents immediately remembered the old hag and the potion. As Anna's first birthday approached, Prince Aron kept debating whether he would go to repay the old hag for the potion as they had agreed.

Eventually the time came for Anna's birthday and the royal palace was preparing for the festivities. Aron had a sleepless night before the celebration, unable to decide whether he should go and pay the old hag, as he had promised, or whether they had been duped, and their daughter's beauty was unconnected to the potion. In fact, everyone remarked at the similarity in beauty between Anna and her mother. Exhausted from lack of sleep, Aron eventually decided that he did not need to pay the old hag. While he spoke decisively to his wife about his decision not to pay the old hag, in his heart Aron felt troubled and unsure. Yet, he stood fast in the face of his uncertainty. Anna's birthday was joyful and the whole kingdom celebrated. She was regarded by all as the most beautiful child in the land.

When night fell, and Anna's parents finally went to bed, Aron's sleep was troubled. He was plagued with the image of the old hag, reminding him of his promise. Aron tossed and turned all night, unable to rest. He heard whispers that if he failed to keep his promise he would be doomed to roam the earth, cast out in Never-Never Land, a place where he would never rest due to his uncertainty. In the morning, he spoke to his wife about his sleepless night, his nightmare, and the lingering fear that he may end up in Never-Never Land. His wife scoffed at this as superstitious nonsense. The princess was certain that Anna was their daughter and not the daughter of the old hag. Despite the potion, she believed strongly that Anna was their daughter and it was important that Aron also stayed true to this belief.

Aron tried hard to draw strength from his wife's strong words. He attempted to repeat her words to himself to stay strong and certain;

however, the fear and uncertainty in his heart would not abate. As the days and nights passed, Aron's doubt grew more and more. He was unable to rest or sleep at night. He wrestled with this uncertainty until one night, in a trance, he left the palace and walked and walked, eventually ending up in Never-Never Land. There he languished, plagued by his uncertainty and the fact that he had not kept his promise.

*When the palace discovered the prince's absence, soldiers were sent to scour all four corners of the earth. Alas, try as they may, they were unable to find the prince. The whole kingdom was in mourning, unsure what had befallen the prince. However, his wife understood what had transpired. She knew that although he was lost and alone, if he only listened to his heart, he could remind himself that Anna was **indeed** his daughter, and that he was the only father she would ever have. The princess knew that if Prince Aron could only remember these things he would find his way out of Never-Never Land and return to his rightful place. So, she lived in the hope that one day he would regain his strength and courage to reclaim what was his.*

Months and years went by, and the princess had to learn to live without her husband, and Anna without her father. However, the courtiers could see the mounting sadness and melancholy growing in Anna's face. They continued to report this to the princess, so one day Anna's mother took Anna to the palace garden and told her that she had arranged for Anna to speak with a wise woman who had the power to answer questions that most found difficult. The princess assured Anna that she could ask the woman any question regardless how difficult it might be. Anna's mother then left the garden, and after a few minutes a wise woman with a warm smile entered and greeted her. Anna was unsure what she was to do and didn't know where to start. However, the warm smile from the wise woman encouraged Anna to begin asking questions that she had always kept to herself. She asked, "Where is my father and why is he not here with me?" *The wise woman paused and then answered,* "Your father is lost and uncertain. Because of this, he is travelling in Never-Never Land. He is there, and not in his rightful place here with you and your mother, because he doubts whether he in fact is really your father, or whether you are the child of the old hag who gave him a potion before you were born." *At this disclosure, Anna asked about the old hag, who she was, and about the potion. The wise woman then explained how Anna's parents met, how they came upon the old hag who sold potions and salves, as well as the promise her father had made to her. With this, Anna became very confused and asked the wise woman,* "So, who is my father and mother? Is the old hag my mother, and is my father really my father?" *In response, the wise woman immediately replied,* "Your father is the only father you have, and your mother is the only mother you have!" *However, still confused, Anna said,* "So why doesn't my father know what is true and what is not true? Why does he not believe that he is my father, and will he ever return home to be with me?" *To this the wise woman replied,* "Your father is plagued by fear and uncertainty which keep him in Never-Never Land. He needs to believe in himself and the fact that he and your mother made you together. Once he believes this and his heart becomes stronger, he will find his way out of Never-Never Land and return home. This is not something that anyone else can do for him. One day, he may decide to find his way back!" *With this, the wise woman said her goodbye to the girl and left the garden. Anna then noticed that her mother had returned, and she ran to her mother, to give her the biggest hug that she had given in a very long time. Anna's mother held her close, and then, looking her in the eye, noticed a smile and warmth in her daughter's face that had not been there for some time.*

Having prepared this fairy tale for the next session with Cynthia and Lexie, I printed two copies so that at the end of the session they could each take one. However, when I went to the waiting room to greet Cynthia and her daughter, I was surprised to see Lexie sitting there together with Alison, another woman whom I had not previously met. Alison was a close friend of Cynthia's and she apologized for Cynthia, saying that Cynthia had been offered some relief teaching that morning, which she could not refuse because of her financial constraints. Cynthia had still wanted Lexie to attend therapy, as she had ongoing concerns about her daughter's well being. Alison assured me that Cynthia would definitely attend the next session, and that she had also invited Lewis to contact me to arrange an appointment for himself.

I was perplexed. What should I do? I had planned to follow up on the previous session and then lead into the fairy tale and read it to them, if it was appropriate. Alternatively, I might focus on other issues that they raised in the session and then give them a printed copy of the fairy tale to take home and read together. I wasn't sure what would be best under the unexpected change of circumstances. Despite my uncertainty, I thanked Alison for bringing Lexie to the session, and invited the child into the therapy room while Alison waited. We spent time talking about her school, the weekend, and her friends; Lexie also played with some of the toys in my room. There were a few children's story books among the toys, so I asked Lexie if she liked reading. She said, "*Yes!*" and that she was one of the best readers in her class. With this, I was able to introduce my fairy tale which I said was a little different from the traditional ones, and asked her if she would like me to read it to her.

Expecting her to jump at the offer, I was a little surprised (and disappointed) at the lack of interest in my fairy tale, as she shrugged her shoulders and said, "*I don't know. Maybe!*" Nevertheless, I used this "maybe" as an opportunity to still bring the fairy tale into the equation, so I said, "*So first you can play with the toys, and then I can read you this new fairy tale, and as you are a good reader, you can tell me if this fairy tale is as good as some of the other fairy tales you have read.*" She nodded at this and then said, "*Okay!*" Thus, after engaging her with the toys, to see what play activity might be productive to help me understand the issues in Lexie's life, I took the opportunity to read the fairy tale in my best reading voice for children.

While reading the story, I occasionally looked up at Lexie to observe her body language and her level of engagement in the session. Occasionally I noticed her yawning and shifting position in the arm chair. My critical assessment told me that Lexie was bored and not very interested in the fairy tale. Despite the lack of reinforcement, I soldiered on until the story was finished. By this time the hour was almost over, and before ending the session, I asked her if she wanted to ask any questions about anything in the story. Lexie simply shrugged and said, "*No, not really.*" I told Lexie that I would see her together with her mother at the same time next week, and since Cynthia was not there today, I asked Lexie to take a copy of the fairy tale for her mother. I told Lexie that I wanted her mother to read the fairy tale before the next session. Lexie smiled, nodded and the session ended. I asked Alison to tell Cynthia about reading the fairy tale, and they left my rooms.

Between sessions, Lewis rang to discuss the reasons why I wanted to see him. I explained that I wanted to involve him as

Cynthia had brought their daughter to me for therapy to address concerns about Lexie's emotional well being. I expressed that as he was Lexie's father it was important that Lewis be aware of his daughter's needs, in order to be there for her. Generally, Lewis accepted this rationale in a positive way, and agreed to attend a session. His preference was to attend on his own, rather than with Cynthia, or both mother and daughter. I suggested various possible times; however, none of these times suited. The only time that suited him was one that Cynthia had already booked. Therefore, I suggested that Lewis could contact Cynthia to see if she would agree for them to swap therapy appointment times. Apart from including him in the therapy, it was also helpful to see if Lewis and Cynthia could work together as parents for the ultimate benefit of their daughter.

Luckily, Cynthia agreed for Lewis to attend at the appointment time she had already made. Cynthia arranged an alternative time for her and Lexie to attend. When Lewis attended, he reported that he found Cynthia controlling and intrusive. This had become increasingly more difficult for him and his wife after their baby was born. Lewis felt that the more Cynthia criticized him and his wife, the more he withdrew, and this was his only way of dealing with Cynthia. The issue of paternity arose, and although it had become the sticking point between Lewis and Cynthia, it became clear that this issue would most likely not have arisen if he didn't feel controlled and under attack from Cynthia, although he did question it at times. The most significant thing that I was able to impress upon Lewis was that being a *father* is not about being a sperm donor, but more about *being there as a father* and being part of a child's life. The fact that he was trained in health and welfare studies made it easier to discuss this at both an academic level and an emotional level. At the end of the session he stated that he would attend further sessions to be there for Lexie, as long as Cynthia didn't continue to be so controlling.

Finally, Cynthia and Lexie attended together. Cynthia stated that she was starting to see some positive changes in Lexie's behaviour at home, and she seemed more settled at school. Getting Lexie to school was becoming easier and she was happier playing with her friends. Cynthia acknowledged that she had become more critical of Lewis and that it was difficult for her to recognise the impact that her criticism of Lewis had on his availability to Lexie. I thanked Cynthia for her willingness to ask Lewis to attend sessions, as well as her flexibility in shifting her appointment with me to accommodate Lewis attending a session.

Although I didn't immediately ask Cynthia whether she had received and read the fairy tale, I was surprised that she didn't mention the story. In some ways I was disappointed that my hard work in writing the fairy tale wasn't acknowledged. I waited to see if she would say anything about the story and whether she had read it. We stayed with the agenda that Cynthia was following, until towards the end of the session, I asked, *"By the way, did Lexie give you the fairy tale I asked her to give you, and have you read it?"* Cynthia replied, *"The fairy tale? Oh wow! That was amazing! I couldn't believe it! It made such a difference. Thank you, it has helped me a lot!"*

The session ended, and subsequently, Cynthia and Lewis attended for several joint sessions. Over time, the issue of the DNA test gradually faded into the background and they focused on how they could parent Lexie. Although Cynthia's colourful language and descriptors of Lewis did not totally abate, towards the end of sessions, the most colourful term she still used was "dickhead", and that was only once! The other more colourful descriptors disappeared. This was quite an improvement and I was thankful for the changes that both parents made for their beautiful daughter!

Although it is difficult to know exactly how the changes in this situation occurred in spite of the intractable situation at the start, it was gratifying that Cynthia consistently demonstrated her availability for Lexie. Also, it was a bonus that Lewis was prepared to attend, notwithstanding his initial unwillingness to be in the same room as Cynthia. These two factors were crucial in creating the possibility for change. Both parents' preparedness to consider focusing on Lexie's needs was of utmost importance in the significant change that occurred. Although fairy tales are often seen as something that interests children, when we are emotionally distressed, we are just grown-up little children. Despite the fact that the issue of paternity and DNA wasn't addressed directly, it seems that the fairy tale had an important input in helping Cynthia to become more open and start to view the situation from a different perspective. Cynthia was able to consider that *Lewis* had a problem with *his* doubts and uncertainty, rather than the fact that he didn't necessarily want to be Lexie's father. I believe this helped to ease Cynthia's criticism towards Lewis, and in turn made it easier for Lewis to work together with Cynthia as parents. This then provided the security that Lexie needed from both her parents.

Chapter 4
Mary Rex

Mary was a psychologist who came to see me for supervision. She was a mature and competent professional, yet she felt unsure about her ability to work with males. Mary had all the skills and experience she needed to work well with most clients. With males, however, and especially with older males, her self-doubt came into play and she struggled to maintain her direction in therapy. She felt that she gave her power away, not only to older male clients, but also to her same-aged male colleagues. Mary felt that in staff meetings, while she often had good ideas to offer, she held back and allowed her male colleagues to dominate the discussion. Then she would become extremely self-critical for not having the courage to speak up at the time. During one of the supervision sessions, Mary asked whether I would see her as a client, because she wanted to work out why she had this problem. She said that often, during many of the recent supervision sessions, she had contemplated the possibility of seeing me for therapy. Although being an older male colleague, she felt that she could trust me sufficiently to work on this issue. I agreed to see her for a set of ten sessions, with a review at the end of this time.

So, once we started working, Mary announced that I needed to change her invoicing as I had her registered as Mary Rex, which was her maiden name, and in the last eighteen months she had married, and had changed her surname to *Pauvres* (meaning "Poor" in French). Being a student of languages, I was quite intrigued by the two names! As I didn't have much family-of-origin information about Mary, I asked her to do a genogram so that I could have a context about her early upbringing and family background.

Mary was an only child and she described her parents as good people who loved her dearly and were very available to her. They were in their forties when Mary was born. Her father was a country doctor and her mother had been a district nurse. They got married late in life, and after a difficult birth with Mary, they decided not to have any other children. Mary grew up in a small country town until she was about twelve years of age, and then her parents shifted to the city, so that she could go to a school and live together with her parents, rather than having her go to boarding school if her parents had stayed in the country town.

At first, Mary reported an unremarkable upbringing, whereby she felt that her parents were very available to her and she was a compliant child. She said that her parents were very reasonable, and she didn't recall any issue of discipline with her parents. They were both quiet and reserved in public, and she remembered that they were affectionate towards her until her first year in primary school. However, Mary started to recall that the physical show of affection seemed to stop once she started Year one at school. Also, I noticed that the genogram was quite thin, with little detail about relationships, connections between people, as well as the fact that there were so few people in her genogram. This paucity of detail in her genogram intrigued me, as Mary had demonstrated considerable creativity in discussing her cases in supervision. She was extremely gifted in helping her clients develop and then explore their genograms. When I raised this issue, she was surprised, saying, *"Well neither of my parents had siblings and my grandparents weren't around much because we lived in the country. We just had friends of my parents who came around. Otherwise that was it as far as family."* Nevertheless, at the end of the session, I asked her to revisit the genogram to see if there was anything else she could add to it between sessions.

At the next session, Mary arrived rather tense. I noticed this and asked her what was up. She paused, and then said that she had a bad week. Her marriage was starting to show cracks in it, and she said that she had the most terrible sleep in ages. In enquiring about her sleep pattern, Mary said, *"You asked me to review the genogram I brought in last session. I did this, and I realised that there were several friends of my parents that I remember calling 'uncle', but they weren't actually related. One of these 'uncles' was uncle Des. He was an old friend of my father. Apparently, they grew up together, and he would often come and visit us when we lived down south. He always brought me sweets and little gifts, and I used to look forward to him visiting. He made me feel special. However, once I remembered about uncle Des, that night, I had the most awful dream. I'm not sure if it was actually a dream, or a memory. Anyway, whatever it was, I remembered that when I was about five and a half, it was before I started year one at school, something happened."* At this point, she paused, and laboured to breathe properly. After a few breaths, she continued, "*My parents had to go to help a woman on a farm, who was in labour. As Uncle Des was visiting, my dad asked him to look after me while they were away. Uncle Des agreed, and I remember him playing with me various games. At first it was fun, but after a while I didn't enjoy what he was doing, and I started to cry. Instead of stopping the game, he just continued the game and then it got worse. He said it was a grown-up game and I would like it, but somehow, I knew that it wasn't a nice game. Anyway, I feel awful right now even thinking about it. I just hated what he made me do, and I don't even want to think about it.*"

At this I said, "*Mary, you don't have to say any more about this if you don't want to. Just trust yourself. If you feel you want to stop there with this, then do so. However, if you want to slow down, breathe, and you do want to say anything else, you can do so, totally at your pace.*"

Mary focused on her breathing for a minute or two, and then said, "*No, I know that it is difficult, but I also realised this week that I have pushed this down, and I'm sure that it's connected with the reason I started this work with you. I'll keep going.*" I reassured her that she could keep going, but that if she needed to slow down or stop at any moment, all she had to do was to say she wanted to stop. Or, if that was difficult, she could raise her hand, and I would stop the session. So, sucking in more air, Mary continued, "*After my mum and dad returned, mum could see that I had been upset. So, she asked me why I was upset, and was it because I had missed them. I didn't know what to say. Although I really didn't understand what uncle Des made me do, I knew that it was wrong, and I wanted to say this, but couldn't. I do remember saying to her that uncle Des had 'hurt' me, but mum just scoffed at that and said, 'Don't be silly. Uncle Des loves you. He would never hurt you.' And with that, I never said another word. I think I decided that from then, I wouldn't let a man touch me, or make me do things. That's when somehow, dad stopped being as affectionate. I'm not sure if he stopped being affectionate, or he picked up something in me that made it difficult for him to be affectionate.*"

After another pause, Mary continued, "*And the thing with my husband this week was connected to this. While I was trying to sort all this out in my head, I tried to tell him about this, but he seemed uninterested, which really upset me. But the thing that made it worse was that at bedtime, he became sexually aroused, and started touching me, and then wanting me to do stuff... you know.... Stuff that reminded me of what uncle Des had made me do.... And I got really angry and pushed him away. It just brought the memory back and I felt repulsed. I couldn't explain what was happening, but then again, I thought, I shouldn't have to explain. If he loves me, he should realise something's happening and he should show some care and concern. So, I didn't do what I am used to doing when I'm involved in conflict. I didn't apologize or back down. He just got into a shitty mood, and he hasn't spoken to me since then."*

By the end of this, I could see that although Mary was exhausted at one level, she also seemed more alive and energetic than I had ever seen her during the previous, numerous supervision sessions. She seemed calmer and more intact within herself than she had been at the beginning of the session. We paused, as neither of us had anything more to say at that time. She sat quietly for a few minutes. All I could say was to thank her in trusting me with what she shared during the session, and while I wanted her to do something further about what she had disclosed, it could wait until our next session. Also, I asked Mary to journal if there were issue that came up between sessions. Mary nodded in agreement and reached out with her hand. I took her hand and held it in both my hands for a minute and the session ended.

The following session, Mary arrived looking calm. She said she had a good week, even though the situation with her husband had not improved. She felt that the cracks in the marriage were getting bigger and she was pessimistic about their future together as a couple. Mary brought in her genogram and said that she had thought a lot about her life, her upbringing, and also about her life as a young adult. Mary said she wanted to talk about her life as an adult, her first marriage, and about what was happening in the present one. I wondered whether this was her way of avoiding talking about the trauma issues which she brought up last session. However, I chose to follow the track that Mary wanted to take.

Mary had been married previously, but her husband had died in a motor vehicle accident about ten years ago. She hadn't wanted children, and after her husband's death, despite the grieving, she developed a good life, feeling contented with a solid base of women friends who were very supportive. For several years she had no thoughts about any romantic relationships. However, about two years ago, a girl friend convinced her to go on a date with her partner's best friend, who was ten years older than Mary and twice divorced. Although Mary said that at first there wasn't any great attraction, she gradually realised that not having a partner, she was going to end up rather lonely, compared to most of her women friends who were in relationships. Therefore, Mary continued dating, and after a year, she agreed to marry Rodney.

Mary went on to say that as Rodney was considerably older, at times she realised that he was at a different stage in life. While not being a party girl, Mary still enjoyed going out and entertaining friends. Rodney, however, was a home-body and often refused to go out with her. Also, she found that he was rather rigid and controlling. Mary said that for the last few months she had cut off emotionally from him, and even the sexual side of the relationship, which started well, was waning. Mary then raised the issue from the previous session, about his sexual preferences which she found distasteful. She said that in the past week, she realised that Rodney somehow reminded her of her uncle Des. There were several features which were similar: his looks, the fact that when he wanted something, he would push until she agreed. Although he seemed caring, Mary realised that his caring seemed to be there only when he wanted something, and the something was often *"the sex thing"*!

I asked Mary that as she was a psychologist and she worked with many couples, what did she think she ought to do regarding this situation. Mary said that she had given it a lot of thought, particularly over the last week, and she wanted to go for couple counselling. However, she had not yet mentioned it to Rodney, as she believed he would pooh-pooh the idea, saying that all this psychobabble is a waste of time. Then I asked her again, *"So, you don't think he will like the idea? Then, what will you do? Will you allow what you think he will do to determine what you will do? Or will you do what you think you want to do?"* She thought about this for a moment, and then said, *"Yeah! You're right. I usually don't like to upset people, and I usually change what I want to do so that it doesn't upset others. I think I've been doing it most of my life. No, I think this is a really important issue! When I go home tonight, I'm going to confront him and say that I want us to go and see a couple therapist, otherwise I don't see any future to our marriage. Yes, I'm clear about that! I'll talk to Rodney tonight."*

We also discussed whom she might contact for couple therapy. Whilst Mary said she would have liked for them to see me, she realised this would not be appropriate. As I had been her supervisor for some years, and she was now receiving individual therapy from me, she realised that my involvement would not be right for Rodney. Mary said that she would contact a colleague whom she met at a recent therapy presentation, who impressed her, and whom she didn't know personally or socially. That way, if Rodney would agree to attend, it would make the sessions more neutral.

Despite my assumption that Mary might want to avoid getting back to the issue of being sexually abused by "uncle Des", she did raise the fact that we had earmarked that issue to be brought up this session. Mary said that she had thought a lot about what happened, and it was clear in her mind that what she had described to me, did in fact happen. While she didn't blame her parents for what happened, she was aware that they were remiss in leaving her with this man, and she also acknowledged that her mother should have taken more care to listen and understand what Mary, as a little girl, was saying about the fact that *"uncle Des hurt me"*. This was a duty-of-care issue that her mother didn't do well enough.

As we only had a few minutes left of the session, I asked Mary if she would do some writing between sessions. Although I had not explained exactly what I wanted her to write, she agreed. I asked Mary to write a letter to Des. In the letter, I wanted her to tell him what he meant to her. From when Mary first knew him, what it was like when he would visit the family home, and how she felt towards him. I also wanted Mary, now, as an adult, to tell him what he did to her and to tell him what she now thinks of him. I asked Mary to include anything she felt that she needed to say, whether it was something that she had wanted to say before or not. Also, as a mature woman, I wanted Mary to tell him what she believes he needed to do. Mary seemed to take this in, and nodded as I was asking her to do these things. With this, the session ended.

At the next session, Mary came in looking somewhat tired. When I asked her how she had been, Mary said that she had not had much sleep since the last session. She said that she and Rodney had been arguing a lot, and this had made it difficult for her to get to sleep. However, Mary said she felt proud that she had maintained her resolve to let Rodney know that she wasn't happy in the marriage, and that she wanted him to go to counselling with her. Although he wasn't happy to hear this, Mary felt positive about having told him, and she had rung for their first appointment, which would be in two weeks' time. She said that this was the first time she remembered sticking to what she set out to do, even though she felt a strong urge to back down.

I had also noticed that she had some sheets of paper when she entered the room, so I then asked her to tell me what they were. Mary said, rather surprised, *"It's the letter you asked me to write. The letter to uncle Des!"* With this, although she proffered the letter to me, I asked her to read it. At first, she looked rather uncomfortable about reading it. After a moment, however, she put on her glasses, and opened the letter to read it.

It started off: *"Dear uncle Des, I am writing this letter to tell you about what you did to me a long time ago. Although you seemed wonderful to me, and I used to enjoy when you visited us, sometimes, I felt very uncomfortable with you. I didn't know at the time why I felt uncomfortable, because you used to bring me lots of things: sweets, chocolates, toys, puzzles, and other things. But now I remember that you used to touch me in ways that I didn't like. Also, I remember that day that mummy and daddy had to go to Mrs Miller who was having a baby, and you were there to look after me. We played many games, which I enjoyed. I always enjoyed the games you played with me. Dad wasn't the type to play those games, and I looked forward to playing those games when you visited. But that day, after we played some of those games, you told me that you wanted to show me another special game, that only you and I would play, and that I was never to tell anyone about. Not even mummy and daddy. At first, I couldn't understand why I couldn't tell mummy and daddy, if it was such a special game. But when you started to play the game, I felt all goosebumpy all over. I didn't like you getting me to take off my knickers, and then I didn't like you touching me. It felt really bad. But then it became worse when you said you wanted me to touch you. I didn't understand why you were doing it and even though I started to cry, you kept insisting that I touch you. I remember just closing my eyes and I couldn't stop crying. Then, the other thing you wanted me to do. I just couldn't do it. I remember crying and pleading with you to stop, and it took such a long time for you to stop, and then you got very angry with me. Then you told me not to be upset and that this was our little secret and that I was never to tell anyone. When I asked 'why?' you said that I would get into trouble. I didn't understand why I should get into trouble, but it made me scared, because I didn't ever like to be in trouble.*

"What you did was bad. You shouldn't have done it. I was only a little girl, and I trusted you. You were a bad man to do that, but even though I haven't thought about this until recently, I think I have been affected by it ever since. I have always been scared to do anything wrong and getting into trouble. I have also stopped myself from saying what I think with older men. I have felt like I had to work out what they thought, and then do what they wanted, so I didn't get into trouble. That's something that I realised recently, and you are to blame for this. I was also upset when I tried to tell my mummy that you had hurt me, and she didn't believe me. She stuck up for you, instead of sticking up for me. You were a very bad man. I wish you had never done this to me. I don't respect you for what you did."

She signed it off: *"Mary"*.

Mary looked exhausted after finishing reading the letter, and we paused for a bit. Attempting to breathe in synchrony with Mary, I gave her some time as a mark of respect for the brave work she had done. Then I said, *"Fantastic Mary. I really appreciate the courage you had in writing the letter."* Mary said, *"You don't know how hard it was. I called you a few choice names before writing it, but I knew I had to write it. I trusted that what you wanted me to do was right. Now I'm glad I did it."*

Then I said, *"Apart from the writing, just now, when you read it, how did you feel?"* Mary replied, *"I don't know. It was strange. I was sort of scared, but as I kept reading, I felt stronger and more... I don't know, sort of angry with him."* I said, *"Tell me a bit more about the anger."* Mary replied, *"I don't know, but I've always had trouble even realizing that I am angry, but when I was reading I felt my body get tense and my pulse get really strong. Almost like I wanted to punch him."*

At this point I said, *"Mary, you've been doing some great work. It's terrific that you are aware of your anger. You've done a lot today. I wonder if we could stop for today and meet again next week, as I want to go through what you've written, for you to do a little more work on it, to then get your power back as a woman. The power that was taken from you when you were a little girl. Is that okay for you?"* At this Mary nodded and said, *"I'm happy to do whatever I need to do. I trust you."*

I then asked Mary to bring the same letter to the next session and we then ended the session.

In the next session I wanted Mary to go through the letter she had written and edit the letter, to see if I could help her get in touch with the powerful woman in her, instead of now being the helpless little girl that had been wounded many years ago. I wanted her to experience her power and see if she could name what he had done to her. I wanted Mary to confront the "uncle Des" that she had been carrying in her head. The "uncle Des" who had disempowered Mary and until now, still had the effect to disempower Mary when she was confronted with men who reminded her of Des. With this in mind, I asked Mary if we could go over the letter from the previous week. She said that she was okay with this.

Thus, I asked her to go through the letter again, however, this time, I wanted her to consider possible changes to the letter. To be able to do this, I had two pens ready: a red pen and a blue pen. The red pen was to be used to cross out things that needed to be changed, and the blue pen, to be used to re-write that part of the letter. We then started to edit the letter.

Most of the letter was fine. I explained to Mary that I just wanted her to reconsider whatever sections she might want to change, as long as she could be forthright and direct in the letter. I said I wanted Mary to go through the letter from the position of being a strong, competent woman with a great deal of life experience. I wanted her to edit the letter so that it was "**hers**". I was happy to offer suggestions, however, Mary was the one who would decide if any changes were made. I wanted Mary to be in charge! Therefore, we started the process of editing the letter. Mary started reading. Once she read, "*Dear uncle Des...*", and she was about to go on, I asked Mary to stop for a moment and consider these three words to see if they fitted for her. Mary thought for a moment, and then took the red pen and crossed out the words: "*dear*" and "*uncle*", and just left "*Des*". Mary then continued to read the letter, and every so often, she would pause at the end of a sentence, and make eye contact with me. At each time, both verbally and non-verbally, I would turn the decision to her, if she needed to change anything. This continued until towards the end when Mary read: "*What you did was bad.*" She stopped at this comment and said, "*I think I need to change this.*" So,

I responded, *"Why do you need to change this, and how would you change it?"* Mary stopped, needing time to think, and then said, *"Bad is not the word. He wasn't just 'bad'. He was horrible! He was despicable! He was a slime to do that to an innocent little girl who trusted him! He was a paedophile, who was grooming me to trust him, while he wasn't trustworthy. He was a 'worm'. That's the best I can say!"* At that, I asked, *"So what would you write in place of 'what you did was bad'?"* Thinking through what she had said, Mary scratched out in red the original words, and in their place, she wrote in capital letters: *"YOU WERE HORRIBLE! YOU WERE DESPICABLE! YOU WERE A SLIME TO DO THAT! YOU WERE A PAEDOPHILE! YOU WERE A WORM: THE LOWEST OF THE LOW!"* And with that Mary took a deep breath and then looked at me, as I nodded in agreement with her sentiments.

After a few more breaths, Mary continued to read further. When she got to the part that said, *"You were a very bad man. I wish you had never done this to me. I don't respect you for what you did."* Mary looked at me again and said, *"I need to change this too."* Without me responding to her, Mary scratched those word out in red, and with due thought, started to write in blue: *"You were a worm. The lowest form of life. You had no right to hurt me like that. I know that you are dead, and if you weren't dead, I would come and tell you what a scum you were!"* With that Mary took a few deeper breaths, and sat back in her chair as if to signify that she had done as much as she needed at this time. We sat quietly for a few minutes to honour the moment for the work Mary had done.

At the following session Mary was quite upbeat. She appeared to have a lot more energy than in previous sessions. I remarked about her energy, and she said, *"You know, I'm starting to get back some enjoyment in life. My work is going well, and I feel much more confident."* I asked what had happened regarding couple therapy and Mary advised me that they had started, but she wasn't sure how motivated Rodney was. She said, *"When the therapist asked Rodney what he wanted to achieve by attending therapy, all he said was that he had only come because I threatened him with divorce. Instead of feeling guilty and trying to encourage him so he would participate, I just kept myself together, and it was interesting watching the therapist do her work. She explored this with him and was able to help him look at what he would want to achieve by coming to therapy. Anyway, I'm still rather pessimistic about whether he will actually take it seriously, but I'm focused on just doing my part and leaving Rodney's part to him."*

I was impressed at the progress that Mary was making. In some ways, I was surprised at her progress and how quickly she was improving. Dealing with a difficult marital situation was already hard to do, let alone doing trauma work at the same time. The fact that Mary was able to integrate the work from the past trauma into her current life (marriage and work), was truly impressive.

I gave Mary the above feedback, as I thought she needed not only to be validated for her courage in pursuing this work, but also to be aware of her progress. I wanted Mary to recognize her strength and have it accessible if she came up against other potentially stressful or traumatic events in this difficult journey she was on. Mary acknowledged this and said she somehow was discovering an internal strength which was new for her, and she felt positive about the future, regardless what life would bring.

Mary then raised the issue that following the last session, with editing the letter, she decided that she also wanted to write a letter to both her mum and dad, about what happened with Des. Again, I was pleasantly surprised at how well she was handling this process. Mary said that she had written the letter to her parents the previous evening, and asked could she read it? I nodded, and she took out the letter and started reading. The letter started with an acknowledgement of what fine parents they were and what a good base they provided for her. She was appreciative of their love, care, and support throughout her life. She said that she would always treasure the parenting she received from them and they were the best mentors a child could have.

Then towards the end of the letter, Mary said, *"Mum and Dad, I also want to say something which happened, that I was not happy about, and I believe, you did not do such a good job about, either. The time when the two of you had to go to Mrs Miller who was giving birth, you left Uncle Des at home to look after me. Although I don't blame you for leaving him to look after me, because you trusted him and he was your friend, I do resent that after you came back and I was very upset, and told you that he had hurt me, you said, 'Don't be silly, Uncle Des wouldn't hurt you.' How could you say that? Why didn't you listen to me? Why didn't you ask more, to find out what happened? What you did, by saying that I was being silly, ended up with me learning to keep my feelings all inside, and not to trust others with very personal things. It also made it hard for me to feel that I could be physically close to you, Dad. Also, as an adult I've found it hard to trust men, especially older men, and I have found it hard to give my opinion when males are around, for fear that I would not be listened to. I'm not blaming you for all this. I'm saying it because I love you dearly and I want you to know what happened and how it affected me. I also wish I could have told you this when you were both alive. However, I'm glad that finally I can tell you. I also want to tell you that I'm doing something now to overcome some of the effects this has had on my life. Just remember that you are both precious to me, I thank you for everything you did for me and I love you dearly."*

Mary sat quietly after reading this letter. I waited for her to be in a state to be able to speak. Eventually, she said, *"What do you think about my letter? Is it okay?"* I said, *"You wrote the letter, and you've just read it. Do you think it's okay?"* Mary said, *"Yes. I think I needed to write it. I needed to get this off my chest, and also to talk to my mum and dad as an adult. I just knew it was important for me to get this stuff out, once I started remembering about Des. It feels okay for me."* With this I said, *"Well, that's the important thing really. You're the one who needs to determine what is okay and what is not okay."*

Following this session, Mary attended for another four sessions with the focus being on consolidating the work she had started with me, on maintaining her self-belief and being able to express her ideas, regardless who was there. She continued to gain strength and self-confidence. Mary became more confident at work and even offered to provide a staff training session on an area of expertise in her work, for which she was highly commended. Mary continued to attend couple counselling with her husband and at the last session it was unclear what would happen to their marriage. For a while, I remained in the dark about that, since when she stopped therapy, she also stopped supervision.

Then, about a year later, Mary contacted me again to ask for some supervision sessions. When she made these appointments, I noticed that she gave my secretary her name as *Mary Rex*. At the first supervision session, I raised this issue about her name and Mary said that she had separated from Rodney. He was doing some individual therapy, and she had decided that she was not prepared at present to stay married to him. They agreed to separate and after another six months they would review their situation and then decide what to do longer term. However, irrespective of the decision, she had decided to revert to her maiden name, *REX*. Mary said, *"I didn't understand why I felt uncomfortable about taking on Rodney's surname after we married. I just felt really uncomfortable. Recently I realized that from when I took on his name: PAUVRES, I actually felt "POOR", just like the name. I always felt okay with the name REX. Rex means King. That feels good. So, I decided to get myself back together!"*

Mary's story demonstrates how trauma from very early times can lie apparently dormant to the person's awareness, yet have significant impact on the person's life, despite the person appearing able to function well in most respects. It also illustrates the incredible strength and resilience Mary had in starting to face the demons that she was not consciously aware of, yet was affected by. Mary had the courage to take the plunge and ask for therapy, instead of simply staying at the *"supervision level"*, which could have enabled her to distance herself from her internal feelings. Mary was aware at some level of her difficulties, but she didn't know how these feelings were connected to her early experiences. Also, despite her difficulties with "older males", Mary trusted me to assist her, and she just needed a head start, to help her to do the work she needed to do to heal the past trauma, and to use her courage and strength to face her current struggles. Mary's courage and resilience were integral in her healing.

Chapter 5
Berryl: Part of the Furniture

On a cold winter's afternoon, Dianne, a young, enthusiastic psychiatric registrar rang, following a seminar she attended, exploring "systemic ways of working with psychiatric patients". She started the conversation thus: *"Hi Aldo, it's Di here. I have been enjoying attending your seminars on systemic ways of working, and it has opened my eyes in my work here at the hospital, and I wanted to ask you a favour."* At this point, although quite pleased to hear she was enjoying the seminars, I was experienced enough to also be aware that it was important not to get seduced into agreeing to do anything before being clear about what I was being asked to do. In response I said, *"Thanks Di. It's good to hear that the seminars are useful, and I've appreciated you putting time during your lunch breaks to attend the seminars. Regarding the favour, if I can, I'd be happy to consider it. What is it?"*

After a pause, Dianne said, *"You probably think I'm crazy here, but I wanted to refer a patient on my team, to see you for individual psychotherapy. I know that as you are not on the same team as me, you don't have to accept the referral, and you will probably think that the person I want to refer is not suitable for psychotherapy. However, I've thought about it a lot for some time. I would really appreciate if you would consider taking on this person for individual psychotherapy. I really think she could benefit. Anyway, please don't feel that you are obliged to take her on!"* I thought, "What a request! Who is the person she wants to refer, and how can I refuse?" I therefore asked, *"Who is the person you want to refer?"* There was a pause and then Dianne said, *"Berryl!"* My jaw dropped. Berryl? You've got to be joking! While I had never formally met Berryl in my three years' working at the hospital, I knew who she was. Everyone who worked at the hospital knew about Berryl. She was an icon in the hospital. Her claim to fame was that she had been an inpatient for about twelve years, and in that time, she had had two periods of leave from the hospital: one was on weekend leave about nine months after first being admitted, and the leave lasted about twelve hours; and the second was again an aborted weekend leave about a year later which lasted about two hours.

I was dumbstruck! What could I say? While I knew I could politely refuse and use any one of many excuses, in reality, I felt obliged to accept the offer, especially as during the seminars I had always stressed that no matter what the diagnosis, there was a human being there, and it was important not to depersonalize the patient by being centred on the diagnosis or the symptoms. Therefore, I thanked Dianne for thinking of me in referring Berryl. I also said that I wasn't sure in what ways I might be able to assist Berryl, but that I would be happy to meet with Berryl and then clarify if I believed that I had something to offer her, and if Berryl wanted to attend sessions. Dianne thanked me, and said she would speak with Berryl and get her to contact me to arrange a meeting time.

A few days later, the charge nurse from the ward that Berryl was on, contacted me to arrange an appointment for Berryl to see me. Although I generally asked for the client to make her own appointment, I confirmed the appointment to see Berryl at the appointed time directly with the nurse. When Berryl finally arrived at my office, which was located in a building adjoining the ward where she had spent the better part of twelve years, she was accompanied by one of the ward nurses. Although I knew what she looked like, I had never taken the time to "look at her". Berryl was a woman in her forties, even though she looked much older and more worn from the ravages of life. Her hair was cut short and had little shape and texture. Berryl shuffled into the room, typical of the psychiatric patients who had been on a vast cocktail of anti-psychotics over many years in the 1970s and 1980s.

I greeted Berryl by reaching out to shake hands as I said hello and said my name. She responded limply by offering the tips of her fingers of her right hand as she said hello, saying her name in a slow, laboured manner. I offered Berryl a seat in my therapy room and thanked the nurse for accompanying her to the session, telling the nurse that we would be roughly an hour, and that I would accompany Berryl back to the ward at the end of the session. This was a most difficult session, with me doing my best to be as client-centred as I could be and to try and establish some sort of rapport with Berryl. Just getting very basic information was very difficult. My questions were met with vast pauses and monosyllabic responses. There was very little flow of dialogue and it felt more like an inquisition, with Berryl having to be on guard, not to give too much away. It was one of the longest therapy hours that I can remember. Towards the end of our time, I asked Berryl the most important question of an initial assessment: *"So Berryl, if you were to come along to other sessions with me, what would you hope to get out of the sessions? What would be helpful?"* To this question Berryl replied with: *"I don't know!"* This would become a standard, stock answer for Berryl and it frustrated me greatly throughout the course of therapy.

Try as I may to ask the question in different ways, I got very little traction in getting Berryl to develop some goals for therapy, so that we could then develop a plan of how we could work together to achieve these goals. What do you do with *"I don't know?"* Fortunately, or unfortunately, I suggested to Berryl that I could see her for eight sessions to explore things, and from there we could do a review. Berryl's response to this was: *"If you want to!"* This was also another of Berryl's stock answers to questions and statements put to her. So, the first session ended there, and we booked weekly sessions for the next seven weeks. After accompanying Berryl back to the ward, I kept wondering, *"Why oh why? Why did I agree to see Berryl? Why did I not leave the decision about what Berryl may want out of attending therapy to her? Why did I not put the onus on Berryl to decide if she wanted to come to sessions or not, instead of me offering to see her for eight sessions?"* I was frustrated with myself for doing the opposite of what I was preaching to my supervisees, and at the same time, not entirely sure why I was letting myself get caught up in doing things that conflicted with my professional beliefs.

There was a wad of case notes about Berryl on the ward. It would have been possible to get a summary of her relevant history from the notes; however, it was important for me to *"meet"* Berryl, and to get an understanding directly from her about her life, who she was, and what was important to her. Generally, with most clients who had some motivation to attend therapy, this would be easy enough to do. However, with Berryl, this was incredibly hard work. Starting with the first session, getting a flow of dialogue happening was difficult. My questions and responses which generally helped the therapy conversation to flow somehow fell flat with Berryl, and getting any sort of detail from her was like extracting teeth. It was slow, awkward, and painful. The therapy hour seemed to drag, and it felt like such hard work. From that very first session, I became aware that instead of looking forward to the forthcoming session, I was dreading the session and anticipating all the possible difficulties that I would encounter.

Despite all this, and in time, I was able to get a reasonable picture of Berryl's life. It seemed that she struggled academically and socially as a child and as an adolescent. Finding study difficult, she was encouraged by her parents to go to business college from the age of fifteen. There, Berryl was able to complete a Certificate in Office Work. Once completed, she was encouraged to get unpaid work experience. Gradually Berryl was able to show sufficient promise and commitment that her employer agreed to give her a full-time job. Berryl was very appreciative of this and was diligent and thorough in her work and in time became a valued member of staff. Through her workplace, Berryl met a young man named Robert, who courted her and after a long engagement, they married. Although they wanted children, Berryl had difficulties conceiving. Eventually they sought medical help to see if they could have a baby; however, before any medical treatment was given, Berryl conceived spontaneously. Berryl and Robert were over the moon. When Berryl was describing this period in her life, she became the most animated I saw her during any of the sessions with her.

Despite the excitement and joy of the pregnancy, in the final trimester Berryl developed toxaemia and needed to be hospitalized. The obstetrician was very concerned for both Berryl and the baby. Despite the concern, the hospital treatment was successful and Berryl eventually had a spontaneous vaginal birth. She had a baby girl whom they called Alice. Although Alice was a healthy child, Berryl struggled with breastfeeding her. She found all the normal adjustments to first-time parenting difficult and soon became overwhelmed and depressed. As things started to get on top of Berryl, she was subsequently diagnosed with post-partum depression and was hospitalized. Despite whatever treatment she received for this, it seems that things got worse and she was then diagnosed with post-partum psychosis. She was hospitalized in the mother-and-baby unit of the psychiatric hospital, to help her establish a secure attachment with the baby.

Unfortunately, it seems that Berryl's psychotic symptoms and general inability to attach to Alice made it difficult for the hospital staff to feel that this was beneficial for the baby's development and Berryl was transferred to the normal section of the psychiatric hospital and the baby was taken home by Robert. Alice was initially looked after by Robert, who was able to arrange time off from work. However, as Berryl's condition deteriorated, eventually Robert's employer put pressure on him to return to work to maintain his position. The only way Robert could do this was to ask Berryl's older sister Susan, who was childless, to look after Alice. For several months, Susan was agreeable to care for Alice, and to bring her to visit Berryl in the hospital regularly. However, this became difficult for Susan to maintain, as Berryl continued to deteriorate as the psychotic symptoms increased.

After more than six months that Susan became the primary caregiver for Alice, two unexpected events took place. First, Robert had reduced his visits to see Berryl, citing the need to spend time with Alice as the reason. Obviously, Berryl felt more and more rejected and marginalized. Then, after more than eight months of Berryl's hospitalization, Robert stunned Berryl with the announcement that he wanted to separate. Berryl went into emotional chaos, assuming that he was having an affair with her sister. Although he denied this vehemently, there was nothing he could say or do to change her belief system.

The second unexpected event which occurred around the same time as the issue of separating took place, was just as catastrophic for Berryl as the first. On one of Susan's visits to the hospital with Alice, Susan announced that she could no longer look after Alice. This further fuelled Berryl's paranoia regarding Robert having an affair with Susan.

Initially Berryl went into emotional chaos. However, when Berryl was lucid enough to reason with her sister, she tried to negotiate to see if there was any way that she could offer her sister money or other inducements to continue looking after Alice until Berryl was well enough to be discharged from hospital. Susan used this bargaining to offer a possible solution: that she would be willing to look after Alice on a permanent basis, if Berryl was prepared to agree to Alice being formally adopted by Susan and her husband. This further exacerbated Berryl's paranoia and psychotic symptoms. Due to this, her hospital stay extended much longer than originally expected and she was finally deemed to be incompetent in making rational decisions for her well being.

Therefore, within a very short space of time from the joy and excitement of marriage and then pregnancy and birth, Berryl's life spiralled into oblivion. She went from joy and happiness to the total loss of everything in her life: her health, her marriage, her baby, her home, and the total control of her life. Robert filed for separation and subsequently for divorce. Despite Berryl's "psychosis and paranoia", it eventually emerged that Robert had started an affair with another woman during Berryl's early hospitalization, and he eventually married this woman about a year after the separation date. Robert also signed the agreement to have Alice be formally adopted by Susan and her husband. With the divorce, Robert subsequently sold the family home, and there was little equity in the home for Berryl.

It took most of the eight sessions to glean this information from Berryl. As a therapist, I found it incredible to observe the dissonance between Berryl describing these tragic events in her life, and the lack of affect her body demonstrated when she was describing these events. I assumed that either she had learnt to switch off all feelings in her body, or that the many years of psychiatric medication her body had absorbed, and the various other treatments, including many courses of electro-convulsive treatment, had anaesthetized her neural receptors, or, finally, that she had totally given up being "*alive*".

Berryl's story emerged in fits and starts, like scattered pieces of a puzzle. Also, the story wasn't presented in a clear, sequential way. It occurred in an itsy-bitsy way, where it was difficult to easily obtain quality information about each event. At times it was difficult to know whether she purposely withheld information until it was asked for, or whether she was so cut off from her experience and pain that the connections did not register in her. Nevertheless, despite how hard the sessions were for me, through this journey, I felt a strong empathy towards Berryl and the trauma she had endured as she slowly described these losses.

As mentioned previously, I found the sessions difficult and from the beginning, not only did I not look forward to each session, I in fact dreaded each upcoming session, anticipating the slow and laborious pace of the session, and the fact that I seemed to be doing most of the work, filling in the spaces between the "I don't know" and the "If you want" statements with which she punctuated the many silences during the sessions. As hard as I seemed to work in the sessions, Berryl appeared to maintain her position of being present physically, but absent emotionally. At the end of the sixth session, I reminded Berryl that we had two further sessions scheduled, and that it would be useful for her to ensure that if there were things that she felt were important to explore in the remaining sessions, to raised them in the final two sessions. With this, we ended the session.

Knowing that we only had two sessions remaining buoyed me somewhat, anticipating that unless there was considerably more energy in the sessions coming from Berryl, it would be a waste of time continuing therapy. Thus, the time arrived for session number seven. As with the previous sessions, I was not looking forward to another long, laborious, and difficult session. However, I waited and waited — but Berryl did not appear at all. After about ten minutes, I rang the ward to enquire where Berryl was. The nurse who answered advised me that Berryl had gone on an excursion with the other patients on the ward, and would not be back for several hours. I found myself feeling frustrated and totally put out, and made this clear to the nurse, who explained that there must have been a mix-up with the change of staff that morning, as Berryl's appointment with me was definitely in the nursing notes. She apologized profusely.

I recall feeling a sense of indignation (*"How on earth can Berryl and the staff treat me so disrespectfully!"*) and self-righteousness, and at the same time a huge sense of relief, that I didn't have to endure another long session where it felt like I was pulling teeth. I found these intense, internal, and conflicting emotions very difficult to integrate. Later that afternoon, I needed to go to another part of the hospital, and on my way, I walked past the bus that was returning the excursion group to the hospital. As Berryl got down from the bus, I waited to get her eye contact, so that I could talk to her. I reminded her that she had missed her appointment this morning, and that we only had one further session booked for the same time the following week. I impressed upon her that this was the last of the eight sessions we had contracted. Again, as I spoke to Berryl, I became aware of the dissonance I felt internally, between the relief of not having to survive the session that morning, and my sense of indignation that Berryl had not attended the appointment. Berryl said she was sorry, as she had tried to tell the nurses that she had an appointment with me, and that she couldn't go on the excursion. However, she said that the nurses would not listen to her, and had insisted that she go on the excursion. In fact, I could understand that this was the way they treated Berryl, as if she was a piece of furniture on the ward, which was just shifted when it needed to be.

The following week, Berryl arrived at the appointed time for her final appointment. In my mind I had a clear plan for the session. I wanted to ensure that we had time for anything that Berryl thought was important to raise, which was *Nothing! We then* reviewed what we had covered during the previous six sessions: *as usual Berryl had almost nothing to offer*. We then had sufficient time to discuss the question of what Berryl wanted to do from here." With this question, Berryl, true to her consistency, had nothing to offer. I felt torn between wanting to make this the final session and not offer any further appointments, as there wasn't sufficient energy from Berryl to continue therapy, and at the same time, feeling sad at knowing what she had been through and wanting to encourage her to continue therapy.

Internally, I agonized over what to do. My head said that unless there was definite energy coming from Berryl to have goals to work on in ongoing therapy, I should not offer more sessions. Yet, Berryl seemed to have so much locked up inside, and maybe therapy could help her unlock this. I felt torn. Nonetheless, I had to make a decision, and when I asked Berryl what she thought should happen regarding either ending sessions or continuing to do some further work together, her standard reply was: *"I don't know. What do you think?"* Rather frustratedly, I told Berryl that unless she had issues that she wanted to work on, I didn't think that it would be useful to continue having sessions. To palliate my discomfort, I also added that since my office was next to her ward, if she changed her mind and decided that sessions would be helpful for her, she could come and see me at any stage, and I would be happy to consider more sessions. With this understanding, we ended the sessions.

I often thought about Berryl and wondered how she was going, while at the same time, I was relieved that I didn't have to endure more excruciating and slow, painstaking sessions trying to get her to talk. I worked at the hospital for another eight months, and during the remainder of that time I had no further direct contact with Berryl. On resigning from that position, I said my goodbyes to the significant people at the hospital and I made a point of also saying goodbye to Berryl. Her response to me saying goodbye was fairly typical, in just shrugging a little, and looked down at her feet as she also said goodbye. That was the last direct contact I had with Berryl. I then went on to develop my private practice, while also doing some work at the Multicultural Psychiatric Centre.

About three years later, on a Friday afternoon, I happened to be home unexpectedly, and I received a telephone call. On picking up the phone I said, *"Hello, Aldo here, who's speaking?"* There was silence. I waited a little and then repeated, *"Hello, Aldo here, who's speaking?"* Again, there was another pause, and then a voice came through in a slow and laconic way, which I recognized very well: *"You probably don't remember me, but my name is…"* and before she could complete her response, I said, *"Berryl! It's so nice to hear from you!"* She said, *"Oh! I'm surprised that you remember me."* I responded, *"How could I not remember you Berryl. It's so nice to hear from you. Tell me, what are you doing?"* Berryl replied, *"A lot's happened since you saw me last. I've dialled this number more than a hundred times, but have never had the courage to let it ring until today. I have wanted to thank you for what you did for me so long ago."* At this, I interjected, saying, *"Oh goodness, that's fine! I don't know that I did much to help."* Berryl's response to this was: *"Oh, you helped me so much. I felt terrible just watching you, and how hard you worked trying to help me. But I just couldn't help much."* Although I did my best to minimize my input in providing much help during those sessions, Berryl interjected by saying, *"No, I used to watch your face as you tried to get me to talk. You worked so hard, and I just couldn't get things out. It was like I was stuck. I felt so sorry for you and I wanted to thank you for still continuing to see me even though I just couldn't get anything out that I had inside."*

We talked for what seemed a long time, and Berryl was able to explain what had happened to her since I left the hospital. She explained that not long after I last saw her, Berryl's mother died, and left her a large sum of money. Rod, the hospital Welfare Officer, helped her invest the money to purchase a three-bedroom unit. Berryl was making progress in the hospital, and as the psychotic symptoms had not been evident for several years, she was helped to get weekend leave which was successful on several occasions. In the last few years she had formed a friendship with another patient at the hospital named Shirley, and Berryl and Shirley discussed the possibility of Shirley renting a room at Berryl's unit, when they would be finally discharged.

Eventually, both Berryl and Shirley were discharged and despite some early teething problems at both being *"free"*, they shared the unit together for the past twelve months without either having to be hospitalized. Berryl also told me that in the last two months her daughter Alice had come back into her life. Apparently, at sixteen years of age, Alice had become a handful for Berryl's sister and had either moved out or had been kicked out of home. Berryl wasn't sure which. Alice had asked Berryl if she could stay over at her place until she could arrange permanent accommodation. This turn of events was both exciting and stressful for Berryl. She was excited at the prospect of finally developing a relationship with Alice, and at the same time she appeared realistically cautious about the fact that Alice would have a lot of unresolved issues of rejection and abandonment which Berryl would need to face with her in due time.

This telephone call was such a wonderful gift. Despite the fact that Berryl had been unresponsive during the sessions, making it easy to assume that she wasn't emotionally present, in fact she had been acutely aware of what was happening. In her recollection of the sessions, she had complete awareness about what was happening for me. It was just that she couldn't express what was happening on the inside for her. Berryl's feedback was invaluable in helping me understand what happens for some clients whose emotions are blunted rendering them unable to express themselves.

At the end of the call, I said to Berryl that I would welcome a follow-up call from her at a future time. About two months later, Berryl made another telephone call and gave me an update on what was happening in her life. She still seemed able to maintain a functional life outside of hospital. Shirley was still renting a room from Berryl and the two of them were able to support each other. Berryl talked about the fact that Alice had a lot of anger and resentment towards her for relinquishing her to her sister's care; however, Berryl was able to listen to her daughter's anger and pain, without decompensating. I felt honoured to witness what Berryl had achieved despite the significant losses she had experienced. From first knowing her as "part of the furniture", she had evolved into a real great human being. During this call I was able to accept her thanking me, and I felt indebted to her for what she had taught me about humanity.

Berryl's story is very significant in many respects. Although it seemed that she was not *"present"* in the sessions, that her affect was flat, that she appeared to have lost interest and energy in expressing her feeling, wishes, desires and wants, she **actually was** present. Because of her lack of responsiveness, I mistakenly assumed she wasn't "receiving" input. However, what Berryl eventually helped me understand was that she received the input okay, she just couldn't respond. How much of this was due to heavy doses of anti-psychotic medication, or institutionalization, or total loss of control of her life, or other factors, is difficult to know. Nevertheless, despite this, Berryl's ability to *"read"* me was better than my ability to read her. In addition, in retrospect, I realised just how astute was the perception of Dianne, the young psychiatric registrar, in picking up something in Berryl that I and others, were unable to see. We were focusing more on outward behaviour, rather than on seeing the *"human being"*.

Chapter 6
Bitter and Twisted

A colleague contacted me to enquire if I would be willing to see a family over a two-week period, to do some intensive work with them, as some family members were coming from interstate. I said it may be a possibility, and although two weeks would not be a particularly long period, I would first appreciate speaking with the family to see the possible value of providing family sessions for them. I was told that there would be five family members attending. The father lived in New South Wales, the daughter lived in Victoria, and the mother and two sons, all adults, lived in Western Australia. The daughter, Phyllis, was the main person trying to arrange family therapy sessions, and she had the opportunity of being able to take two weeks off and come to WA for therapy. She had convinced her father to come over from New South Wales, and had also gotten an agreement from her mother and middle brother to attend. Her older brother had also agreed to be involved, but she wasn't certain whether he would definitely participate in family therapy.

After the initial discussion with my colleague, who had been contacted by Phyllis' therapist in Victoria, it was left that Phyllis would contact me to discuss whether family therapy was viable. Within twenty-four hours, Phyllis rang and gave me a brief outline of the reasons for wanting family therapy. She stated that she was the youngest of three siblings, and her parents had been separated for about forty-eight years. She also said that at this stage of his life, her father was prepared to confront the issue of his abandonment of the family many years earlier and was prepared to do what he could to facilitate healing between the various members of the family. Both she and her father were prepared to travel to Western Australia for about two weeks to do some intensive work with the family. She was concerned that her eldest brother was not particularly motivated to attend the sessions. Also, she was concerned that her mother wasn't very psychologically-minded and therefore might not get much out of family therapy.

While I would normally see families together over an extended period of time, especially with intense issues which date back many years, I said that I was prepared to see the family intensively over this two-week period, provided they would also consider setting up another period of intensive family therapy some months after the two weeks. Phyllis said she would be prepared to do this, and she thought her father would also be prepared to commit. She wasn't sure about the others. Thus, it was left that we arrange a series of two-hour appointments, probably every second day, over a two-week period. A range of potential dates was discussed, and Phyllis was agreeable to be the one to liaise with the others in the family, to confirm appointment dates and times.

Eventually, about four weeks later, the first appointment arrived. All five family members attended:

Eddie (Father), age: 82 years;

Martha (Mother), age: 82 years;

Thomas, age: 55 years;

Douglas, age: 52 years; &

Phyllis, age: 51 years.

They all arrived a few minutes early, and at the appointed time, Phyllis met me and introduced each of her family to me. We had contracted five appointments each of two hours over the two-week period that Eddie and Phyllis were going to be in West Australia. My focus in the first session was to meet each family member, to "join" with them, and to develop a therapeutic rapport with each. Also, it was important for me to obtain an understanding from each family member about what each saw as the reasons for attending family therapy, as well as what each of the family members wanted to achieve by attending family therapy.

When a family arrives for therapy, often individual members are either interested in getting *"others"* to change, or they are like a man in a female dress-shop: simply there *"visiting"* and not wanting to get too involved. However, if you are fortunate as a therapist, you may occasionally find one family member offering to consider what s/he can do **to change the relationship or dynamic between her/himself and others**. When this occurs, it is a bonus, as it promises the possibility of positive changes. In this session, the most helpful thing that happened was that Eddie took responsibility for saying that he had come to family therapy because he knew that he had done things in the past that had seriously affected each member of his family, and that he wanted to see what he could do to help heal some of the wounds that he had created. As mentioned earlier, this was truly a gift that promised a lot, despite the fact that other family members were not as open to look at what they could each personally contribute to achieving positive changes in the family.

Martha said that the problems of long ago were no longer an issue, and she didn't believe there were any problems to be dealt with at present. She didn't know what all the fuss was about. Her eldest son Thomas wasn't sure that family therapy would be useful to this family. He had agreed to attend one session, but if it seemed a waste of time after the first session, he would not be continuing. He said, "*Some people are never going to change, so what is the value in talking about things if they are so closed off!*" Douglas said that he was prepared to come along to family therapy sessions, but that he did not feel that he had any problems with any of the other family members, so he wasn't sure that his participation was required. He knew that others had many unresolved issues, but he believed that they didn't affect him personally. When asked if he was prepared to attend and contribute to the sessions, he said that he was.

Finally, Phyllis said that she had organized these sessions because she knew that there were a lot of unresolved issues in the family, and she was hopeful that while her parents were still alive, that they might be prepared to heal these wounds. When asked what she wanted from the sessions, she said she wanted to help the others to deal with "*the unresolved stuff!*" She struggled to articulate what she wanted for herself. Most of what she said revolved around every other family member resolving their relationship with another family member, and little to do with her. In summarizing the first session, I explained that my preference was for all five members to attend all five sessions, and I also impressed upon them my belief that the more they each contributed, the better the outcome for all. We then spent the remainder of the session getting each to assist me with a history of the family; how Eddie and Martha met, how they married and came to Western Australia shortly after their wedding, and the remaining history up to Eddie's leaving the family, as well as what had happened since he left, some 48 years ago.

All five family members attended the next session. As we were about to start the session, in the waiting room, Eddie asked if he could have a few minutes with me on his own. Obviously, as I was seeing them in family therapy, I generally would not have considered this appropriate, and it raised my concerns that this could be a ploy to undermine the equity in seeing all members of the family together. With his request, I said to Eddie that generally, I preferred to see everyone together, however, if everyone in the family was agreeable for one member to have some time on her/his own, then that would be acceptable, as long as anything that was discussed individually could then be discussed with all members of the family. Eddie said, with everyone present, that he had asked the rest of the family for permission, and they had all agreed for him to have a little time first on his own. They all nodded in agreement. Therefore, I consented to the request, and Eddie entered the therapy room while the other four sat in the waiting area.

Eddie started: *"There's nothing secret about what I wanted to say to you. I just wanted to get all the facts out, and to take responsibility for my part in what happened years ago."* He then went on to repeat what he and Martha had previously outlined to me about how they first met, fell in love, and then came to Western Australia. Eddie and Martha met at church. Both their families were members of a Christian sect in country NSW, and when they met and fell in love, both families were happy and encouraged them to become engaged and to plan a wedding together. In planning their wedding, the congregation approved of their going to a country town in WA immediately after marriage, as in this town there was a thriving community of their religious group, and work and accommodation were guaranteed. As the elders of the church encouraged this, Eddie and Martha decided that they should follow their advice.

The day after their wedding, they travelled by train, first to Sydney, then from Sydney to Perth, and then by train and bus to their little wheatbelt town, to make their home. They were excited that they were starting life as two missionaries, about to do something great for mankind, and that they had a supportive extended family/community behind them. On arriving in the town, they were shown around to the accommodation that was arranged for them. Eddie had a truck-driving licence and did a lot of work driving between the various country towns, as well as farm work, which he was happy doing. Martha became integrated into the local community, of which more than half the town were members of their religion. They were amazed that although the religious community were very strict about sexual conduct, they noticed that several of the elders, and some of their adolescent children were involved in highly promiscuous activity at night during farm dances. Both Eddie and Martha noticed this, but as they were very much in love and their sexual activity was exclusive of others, they didn't question the hypocrisy that it demonstrated.

Eddie then talked about two incidents that he thought had a lot to do with the deterioration of the relationship between him and Martha. First, after eighteen months, they had their first child: a son named Graeme. He was a beautiful child and they were ecstatic. Their lives revolved around this child and they felt close as a couple and excited at wanting other children. When Graeme was about fifteen months old, Martha became pregnant with their second child whom they eventually named Thomas. By the beginning of the second pregnancy, they had moved to a farm a few kilometres out of the town. Eddie worked six days a week. The only day off was on the day that they went to church. The elders provided Eddie with the work, and a fair amount of his work was done voluntarily for the church. As Graeme grew and started to crawl and walk, Eddie and Martha planned to build a fence around the homestead, so that Graeme could play and run around safely on the property. However, on his free time when he planned to put up a fence, invariably, he was given other, more urgent work for the church to do; therefore, close to the time of Thomas' birth, only part of the fencing around the house had been erected. At that time, Martha's sister Sue had decided to come over together with her husband and son for the birth of Martha's second baby.

A few days before Thomas was born, the two families spent the morning together enjoying each other's company. Later that day, the elders rang Eddie to ask him to do some truck driving for the church. He agreed to do this for the elders, and he took Bill, his brother-in-law, with him. Late that afternoon, when Eddie returned home, Martha and Sue were in a panic. Half the townspeople were there at their home. Nobody could find

Graeme. Apparently, Graeme had been playing on the porch, and while Martha and Sue put Sue's son down for an afternoon nap, they made tea, and then went to the porch to find that Graeme had disappeared. They searched everywhere, calling Graeme, but to no avail. Eventually Martha rang one of the elders for help, as they could not get in touch with Eddie, since in the late 1950s and early 1960s there weren't any mobile phones.

Eddie was beside himself, wracking his brains to work out where Graeme might have gone, or who could have taken him. He eventually raced up the hill to the dam, and there, floating upside down, was his little boy. Eddie felt totally destroyed! And when he came down the hill, carrying the body of his child, all he could remember was the look on the faces of the people. Not only did he feel that life stopped there that day, but later, when Martha was screaming in her distress, his sister-in-law Sue blamed him for the death of Graeme. She said that Eddie was lazy, and he should have put up the fence as he had promised, and if he had done so, Graeme would still be alive. Eddie felt shamed and humiliated by this outburst, but said nothing to Sue and Bill. To this day, Eddie never spoke to Sue again. Although he did not believe he was responsible for Graeme's death, he felt shamed by that accusation which stung him deeply.

The second thing he wanted to get off his chest was the fact that he did, on one occasion, betray Martha. Eddie wanted to tell me the story as it happened, because he felt that the story had been turned and twisted in such a way that many things were said to have happened that didn't actually happen. Eddie also said that once he had told me exactly what happened, he was prepared to go through it with the others. Under these conditions, he started the story. On a cold and very wet winter's day he had to take a load on his truck to another town. Knowing that he was about to drive off to this town, one of the elders asked Eddie to give a young woman a lift in his truck, on his way to a neighbouring town. As it was raining and the elder told him that she had been deserted by her husband, Eddie felt obligated to give her a lift home. Eddie said that he had never met this woman previously, and he agreed to do what the church elder asked. On the journey, the rain came bucketing down, making visibility almost impossible, and the road was just a series of potholes. Eddie had to drive ever so slowly, so it took an inordinate amount of time to get to his destination. Eventually he arrived at her farmhouse and wanted to drop her off quickly to continue his journey. However, she insisted on having him come inside for a cup of tea, as a way of thanking him. At first Eddie refused, saying that it would take him a long time to get the load to the neighbouring town due to the weather. Nevertheless, she insisted that as it was teeming down with rain, if he spent a few minutes having a warm cup of tea, the weather might improve, and he could then drive more quickly to the town.

Thus, Eddie decided to stay for a few minutes for a cup of tea. In going from the truck to the farmhouse, they both got drenched, and as she put the kettle on, she said she was going to her bedroom to change out of her wet clothes. Eventually the kettle was whistling, and Eddie called out to her that the kettle had boiled. However, as the woman didn't answer, he went near her door and shouted out again, to make it easier for her to hear. Instead of responding to this, she called out for Eddie to come into the bedroom. He said that although he was reluctant to do so, she insisted that he enter, and on opening the door, he saw her lying on her bed, naked, with her legs wide apart, beckoning him to come to her. Eddie said he didn't know what to do. This came at a time after Graeme's death, when Martha was grieving and nothing was happening sexually between them, as she was also breastfeeding Thomas, who had been born within a week of Graeme's death.

Although he regrets this to this day, Eddie said that the temptation was too much, and he succumbed to having sex with this woman. Although he enjoyed the sex at that time, immediately after getting back in his truck, the remorse and guilt of what he had done overwhelmed him. Eddie spent the whole trip to the town and back home regretting what he had done. Wracked with shame and guilt, upon returning home he told Martha about the shameful thing he had done. Eddie didn't know what to do and how to atone for this betrayal of trust. Eventually he chose to speak with the elder who had asked him to give the young woman a lift, and he disclosed what he had done. The elder told Eddie not to speak of this to anyone, and he would handle it. A day or two later, the elder asked him to come to a meeting where he and another elder went though the story, and again Eddie was advised not to speak of this to anyone. Eddie waited to hear from the elders, and he told Martha about his talks with them. When it came to the next church service, the service started as normal, but then the elder that he had first disclosed his shame to, got up at the pulpit and said that something terrible had occurred in their congregation. He then named Eddie as a *"sinner and lascivious perpetrator of terrible evil"*, and that the congregation should shun him and his family for the shameful act of fornication that he had committed. Eddie was beside himself. He was unable to speak. Eddie felt totally betrayed by the elder and ashamed to show his face in the community. He remembered getting up from his seat and leaving the church. This was the church that had meant so much to him!

Eddie couldn't remember what happened after that and whether he or someone else took Martha and their children back home to the farm. He said that the period after that was hazy. Eddie did his farm work and truck driving, but he had no contact with the congregation. He was, in his words: *"Sent to Coventry!"* Eddie couldn't remember exactly how much time elapsed between this event and when he finally decided to leave the family. By the time he left, Thomas was five, Douglas was three, and Phyllis was a little over one year old. It seems that life stopped for Eddie from that day at the church. Eddie felt so utterly betrayed that he didn't see the point of living. This was what he had carried with him for nearly half a century, and he wanted to take responsibility for what he did, that had so many ramifications for the others in his family. At this point, I asked Eddie whether it was time to have the others join us, and he said yes.

When the others joined us, I said to Eddie, *"Thank you for sharing what you told me. It's probably best that I get you to recount what you have just gone through with me."* At this, Eddie took over and went through in almost the same degree of detail, what he had disclosed to me. Everyone sat and listened to what Eddie acknowledged as his misdeeds. He was as open about the various events with the family as he had been with me. There were very few questions asked by the family members. The only thing I noticed was Martha's bodily reaction to Eddie's statement that there was *"very little sex after Graeme's death"*. When I commented on her body language and what it meant, at first she minimized it saying that she didn't understand what I meant. However, on my further questioning what her body language was saying, she replied that she found it hard to believe Eddie saying that there was very little sex, yet there had been two other children born following the death of Graeme and the birth of Thomas. Whilst there was some minor arguing around this between Eddie and Martha, Thomas was the one who then entered the discussion about this time, saying that his mother wasn't there for him. She was never there from his birth, and she had not been there for him throughout his life.

By this time, we had gone a few minutes over our appointed time and I wanted to bring the session together and plan for the next session that was scheduled two days later. However, something had been ignited in Thomas and he wasn't ready to end the session. He wanted to talk about how his mother hadn't been there for him. No amount at trying to calm things down was working, so I asked him what he had been carrying inside for many years. He said that he knew from before he could speak, that his mother didn't care about him. Over the years he had tried to be the dutiful son, the eldest, the mentor for his little brother and sister, and all that happened was that he got shat upon! Thomas' final statement to his mother was: *"You were never there! You were just bitter and twisted! No amount of therapy is going to make any difference!"*

The session ended with this intense accusation, and I asked Martha to think about the things that she remembered which didn't correspond to Eddie's recollection of the past, and if she could write these things down, for the next session. Also, I asked Thomas to write down the hurts and resentments he had, not only to his mother, but to other significant people in his life, and to bring what he wrote to the next session.

At the next session, Phyllis opened the conversation. She said that on the weekend, between sessions, she had wanted to spend some time with a childhood friend. However, during the weekend Phyllis said she had a *"Spack-Attack"*. I asked her what she meant by a spack-attack, and she explained that being back "home", staying at her mother's house, had brought up a lot of the same feelings she remembered experiencing when she was a teenager: an incredible need for space and freedom. She had realised during the therapy sessions so far that she had been denying her own needs, by simply focusing on helping the family heal. On the weekend, Phyllis just wanted to go out to dinner with her childhood friend, whom she hadn't seen in years, and had told her mother about going out to dinner. However, the closer it came to going out, the more pressure she felt from her mother to stay home. She couldn't understand what was happening, until she felt the pressure to contact her friend and cancel their dinner. Once she had cancelled the dinner, she just felt a huge rage which she hadn't experienced since being a teenager. It ended in an argument with her mother, with Phyllis driving away, ending up at a pub, getting some alcohol, and ending up sleeping in the car overnight.

While it was distressing for Phyllis at the time, on reflection she said that it had been a very important experience, as she felt it helped her integrate a lot of the therapy she had done over many years. Phyllis said she could now understand why at times she felt feelings which she couldn't connect with, and yet, now made sense. She talked about how what happened on Saturday night, and her mother's response the next morning: totally ignoring and denying what had happened, and the connection of this to her leaving Western Australia when she was nineteen years old, now made a lot of sense. It was as if all the pieces of the puzzle had been connected! Phyllis was thankful that this had happened, and she wanted to use the remaining sessions to look at what she needed to do for *herself*, and not just to fix the family.

When there was an opportunity to ask Martha about her experience of what happened for her over this event on Saturday and Sunday, all she could say was that she didn't understand what all the fuss was about for Phyllis. Martha said that as Phyllis hardly ever returned to West Australia, she just wanted to spend the evening with her, and Phyllis could always see her friend on another visit. Phyllis' bodily reaction was palpable. Although it was all non-verbal and she chose to contain it at that time, she seemed to be seething at her mother's denial of events. Martha, however, was more interested in following up on what I had asked her to think about at the end of the last session. She wanted to talk about the issue of why Eddie left the family, and also her belief that he had more than a single sexual encounter with the woman that he had given a lift to.

Martha believed that Eddie's statement—that there was little emotional and sexual contact between herself and Eddie—

was not true. She reiterated that if this was so, then how was it that they had two more children, Douglas and Phyllis, after Thomas was born? She also mentioned that they had a miscarriage between Thomas and Douglas. She felt that Eddie's recollection of events was not the same as hers. She also questioned the relationship between Eddie and this other woman (by the way, neither of them gave her a name, except "the other woman").

Martha questioned Eddie at this session, as she had been told that when Eddie left the family, he had gone to live in Perth with the other woman. Martha wanted to know if this was true. Eddie reasserted what he had stated previously. He acknowledged the fact that he had sex with her when he dropped her off on that rain-drenched afternoon. However, he was wracked with guilt and shame, and owned up to Martha as soon as he got home. Eddie also acknowledged that after a few weeks that he had left the family and came to Perth, he heard that the other woman had also come to Perth, and he met with her. However, he swore black and blue that there had not been any sexual, or emotional, connection with this woman after he left the family. He hoped that Martha would believe him, as he said that he wanted to do what he could to heal the damage he had created, so there would be little point in lying about this now.

While it was interesting to note that Martha chose not to comment on what Thomas had said about her being "bitter and twisted", it also made sense that much of Martha's life had been dominated by the ethos: "*Grin and bear it, carry on, no matter what.*" Martha stated that after the death of Graeme, she just had to carry on, as she had a little baby and couldn't wallow in her sorrow. She did, however, say that Eddie also just immersed himself in work, and there was little fun or joy in their lives. Martha felt that they just had to keep going and not get stuck in their grief. She said she had learnt that a long time ago, when her little sister died from meningitis, and her mother modelled how to handle this tragedy.

Thomas also wanted to have his say in this session. He said that he had spent a lot of time thinking about how his family had ruined his life. For many years he had blamed his father for abandoning him. For about twenty years, he refused any opportunity he had to contact his father. Thomas resented Phyllis, who was the first to have made contact with her father when she left home and went east. However, on one of his business trips to the east coast some years ago, he eventually agreed to meet his father, and after their first meeting, although he couldn't explain why, he suddenly felt his anger and resentment towards his father dissipate. In contrast with this, however, his intense feelings of hate and resentment towards his mother continued to this day. Thomas felt there was nothing that anyone could do to change these feelings and that his mother was extremely fixed and rigid, and that she was continuing to demonstrate this in the sessions so far.

Thomas felt that when his father left the family, the burden to be the "man of the house" was put on him. He felt a huge weight and responsibility to have to do everything perfectly, but whatever he did was never good enough for his mother. Thomas recalled numerous instances where he tried to be the big brother and the responsible one, yet the effect was that his mother would find something or other to criticize in him. Thomas knew that money was scarce, so at thirteen, he started to get jobs after school and on weekends to help the family. And yet, all that Thomas remembered was his mother commenting that his marks at school were bad. Everything he tried ended up with his inadequacies being noticed and focused on by his mother.

During this session, Douglas, who until now had kept a low profile, said that he had remembered a number of things after the last session. When Eddie had talked about deciding to leave the family, Douglas recalled his father packing two suitcases and putting them into a blue Holden Ute. As he said this, Thomas jumped in, and said, "*How can you remember this? You were too young.*" For the first time, Douglas became very animated and retorted vehemently, "*Don't tell me what I can remember and what I can't remember! I remember this as if it was yesterday. I know what I remember! I know you've got your problems, but you've been controlling me all my life. It's almost as if what you experienced is real, and anything that others experience is not real. Stop telling me what I remember!*"

At this Phyllis chimed in and said, "*Yeah! I also wanted to say something the other day. You said that Mum wasn't there for you from birth. You said you knew this even before you could speak. That was okay for you, because you feel this strongly. Yet, when I have said in the past that all this has affected me, too, your comment was that I was too young to be affected, because I was only a year old when Dad left. How is it that you can remember and be affected from when you were very small, and somehow for me, I was too young to be affected?"*

This intense reaction from both his siblings seemed difficult for Thomas to stomach: both his brother and sister taking him to task at his behaviour. Despite the tension this created in the session, I was pleased to hear both Douglas and Phyllis being prepared to express themselves, rather than take the position of *"not rocking the boat"*. Thomas stopped talking for a while, and the family went quiet.

Phyllis had indicated that when she first rang to discuss the possibility of making appointments, she was intimidated by Thomas and was unable to oppose him in any way. Therefore, for Phyllis to become aware of Thomas' "duality" in having one set of rules for others, and another for himself, and then being able to voice this clearly, was a vast improvement. Also, having Douglas challenge Thomas in an appropriate way was good to experience, for me as the therapist. To give Thomas credit, despite that he may have felt ganged-up on by his siblings, he nevertheless seemed to take the criticism in his stride, and didn't storm off and withdraw from the sessions.

At the end of the third session, as I had previously mentioned writing letters and keeping journals, Martha raised the point that she had written a letter to Eddie many years ago and had never sent it to him. She believed she still had the letter, and asked if could she bring it to the next session if she could find it. I encouraged her to do so after I had checked this out with Eddie. Eddie said that he would appreciate hearing the contents of the letter, and even though he found the emotions he felt the last few days difficult to go through, he believed that Phyllis had done the right thing in organizing appointments for the whole family to attend.

The fourth session largely revolved around Martha's letter to Eddie. Essentially it was written a few months after Eddie had left the family. Martha opened the letter and offered it to me. I said that I preferred her to read it *(when the author of the letter reads it, rather than a third person, the intensity of the feeling expressed in the letter is greater)*. She then hesitated, took a deep breath, put on her reading glasses, and started to read. Apart from saying how each of the children were at the time, in the letter, she had many questions of Eddie. Why did he leave? Had the love between them died? Would he ever come back home? And many, many more questions. It was interesting that she wrote the letter, but never sent it to Eddie. She said that a friend of hers had suggested she write the letter, and even if she didn't send it, it might help her. So, she did decide to write it.

At the age of eighty-two, Martha had finally disclosed these many questions which she had never had the courage to voice over the preceding fifty years. Also, it was interesting watching Eddie as Martha read the letter. There appeared a deep sadness on his face, even though he never interrupted her as she read. At the end of the letter, when asked for his feedback regarding the letter, he said that it was difficult for him to say what he might have done if she had sent the letter to him. Eddie remembered that he was in a dark place when he left the family. Then he changed what he had just said, *"No, not when I left the family — when I "abandoned" the family. "* Eddie said that it was difficult to know how he might have read the letter, as he was struggling with who he was as a man, with his feelings of deep guilt and remorse at letting his family down and with his desperate need to re-construct his life.

The rest of the session was focused on the family members reminiscing about the things that Martha's letter raised for each of them. They were each able to talk about what they remembered from the time Eddie left, as well as growing up in Perth, living in a housing commission home. Also, what it was like feeling alienated from society: they had been ostracized from their community in the country town, and then, coming to the city, they were outsiders, never feeling that they were accepted at school or in the dreadful neighbourhood they were living in. At the end of this session, I asked them to think about the remaining things they still needed to focus on in the final session which was scheduled in two days' time, so that they could get the most out of the sessions.

In the final session I wanted each family member to have an opportunity to give feedback on how the sessions had been for them. I also asked them if they had any other issue that they wanted to focus on before the feedback part of the session. However, each said there was nothing else that was still outstanding. I asked them to reflect on what they initially said they wanted out of the sessions, what they each believed they contributed to the sessions, and what they felt that they each got out of the sessions. I also asked them to consider what they wanted to do after this session. Although this was the final session we had planned, what would they like to do beyond this session, if anything. Each of the family members gave positive feedback about having had the opportunity to talk about things in their lives that had been impossible for them to talk about previously.

Phyllis said that she never imagined that she would have been able to say what she said to her brother Thomas, and that although it had been difficult, she felt closer to him than she had felt previously. She was also surprised that she started the process of family therapy thinking that everyone else in the family needed it, and yet, during the two weeks, she realized that she needed to work on herself more. Phyllis said that going back home, she would do more work with her therapist on some of the issues that came out of this experience, and she realized that she needed to take better care of herself.

Eddie was very emotional at the last appointment, saying that he felt sad at the harm he had caused to his family. He reiterated that he now recognised that he had abandoned his family, even though that was not his intention at the time. Eddie knew that he could not undo what he had done, but for his remaining years, he wanted all of them to know that if he could continue to do anything to make up for what he created, that he was open to do what he could. He was thankful that everyone had taken part in the sessions and if it was relevant, he would make the time to attend family therapy at a future date. Despite the fact that he lived so far away, Eddie said he would return to West Australia if it helped others in the family. Finally, he wished that Martha and Thomas could one day have a good relationship as mother and son.

Martha said that it was helpful to talk about the past, but even before attending, she didn't have any problems, because what happened, had happened so long ago, and she didn't harbour resentments. She believed that she had done what she could to get on with her life. Other members of the family appeared to find it hard to believe this, as they saw this as Martha's stoicism, and they believed that her life had stood still as she never allowed another man into her life, even though she had several opportunities. However, Thomas and Phyllis, who expressed these thoughts, did so in a quiet way, without appearing to contradict or judge Martha.

Douglas expressed gratitude at having had the opportunity to take part, even though at the outset he did not believe that his presence was important. He said that although he didn't say much through the sessions, he had gotten a lot out of the therapy. Douglas realized that he harboured some resentment towards Thomas for dominating him, and through the sessions he became aware that he needed to speak out and assert himself more. He also mentioned that his wife had been telling him this for years, and now he needed to let her know that she was right.

Thomas said that there was a very small change starting to happen. He felt less angry towards his mother and through listening to her letter, he felt more able to see how difficult it must have been for her. He added that, nevertheless, this was a small change, and he would see if this change would grow or not. So Thomas didn't want to get carried away in being overly positive, even though the therapy had been helpful, and he would just wait and see. He would see what the others in the family did in the coming months, to see if this process made any long-term difference.

In discussing what they might do after this series of sessions, they all agreed that they would let the dust settle, and they would keep in touch with each other over the next few months. Depending on what happened, they agreed that family therapy had opened up some of the wounds, and they would each do what they could to try to heal these wounds. Phyllis said that she would still liaise with the others and in a few months consider whether they might have a follow-up set of sessions. The session ended with each hugging each other.

Phyllis offered to continue as the primary contact person to keep me informed regarding the family and to advise me if they decided to resume sessions at a future date. For several months she emailed me, keeping me informed about her contact with the others, as well as about the work that she was doing with her therapist back home. Phyllis acknowledged the benefits of the work done, especially being able to speak up with her brother, and also becoming clearer about her interaction with her mother. In relation to this issue, she said that it had also helped her in her relationship with her young adult son. Phyllis realized after she returned home that her son was expressing a similar reaction to her, that she had recognized that weekend towards her mother. This had been a real awakening for her, and through the therapy she was receiving, she was able to start a process of change in her behaviour towards her son. She felt extremely pleased with herself, for noticing this pattern and being able to make changes at this stage of her relationship with her son.

Although the updates reduced with time, after about nine months, Phyllis emailed me to advise that her father was coming back to West Australia to support Martha in some negative interaction between Thomas and Martha. Phyllis asked if I would see Eddie and Martha together. I explained that I would be happy to see the two of them, or both together with Thomas. I asked that either Martha or Eddie contact me directly to arrange any appointments.

Subsequently, Eddie and Martha attended two sessions together. The main focus was still on the resentment that Thomas held towards his mother. Eddie and Martha said that they had invited Thomas to also attend, but he had declined. By the end of the second session, it seemed that Eddie had been able to talk to Thomas, and despite some ongoing tension between mother and son, they were back to talking to each other, and Eddie felt that he would stay for another short while before returning home.

The last email contact I received from Phyllis was about six weeks later. Apart from updating me about her progress and the improvement in her relationship with her son, as well as with her husband, she went into great detail talking about her father and mother. Phyllis stated that when her father had last come to Western Australia, Martha had encouraged him to stay at her house. From Phyllis' telephone contacts with her father and mother, she felt that a "relationship" was being rekindled between them. She said that while she was aware that it might be her fantasy, she believed that Eddie and Martha had somehow reconnected. Phyllis said that although it might not lead anywhere, she was confident that they were talking to each other in the way a young couple talk when they are courting!

That was the final contact I had with Phyllis and her family. Regardless of whether Eddie and Martha had started to develop something with each other, or not, after nearly half a century, some things seemed to have changed. Through the process of family therapy, Eddie was able to demonstrate great strength in taking responsibility for his part in significantly affecting his family. He was able to show his regret and take responsibility for the things he had done, and his actions helped others in the family to heal. Eddie's acknowledgement that he abandoned the family demonstrated incredible courage. Phyllis was able to grow up emotionally and recognize the effect her mother had had on her, and face her mother, more as a woman than as a girl. In addition, she was able to use this knowledge to change the dynamic between her and her son. There was also some healing and more openness between all the family members, including the three siblings.

Although some things may have not changed appreciably, with only ten hours of family therapy over a two-week period, this family was able to make significant changes that did not appear possible at first. It took great courage and resourcefulness from all five family members to agree to attend such an important series of brief family therapy sessions. I felt privileged to have been part of this process of change, as my part was just to be there and to facilitate the conversations.

Chapter 7
Jesus Travelled through the Desert

Summer had come early, and it was unusual that at this stage of the year we had several days of over 35 degrees celsius. On one particularly hot, 40-degrees-celsius day, a psychiatric nurse on the hospital ward asked me for help with a recently admitted Italian patient. I was told that she had been hospitalized because she was psychotic and uncommunicative. It seemed that the staff didn't feel that they could get through to her, and they could not get her to take in any fluids. They had little background about this woman. Her husband spoke little English and they were unsure whether she spoke English well enough to understand what they were saying.

When they pointed her out to me, I was concerned that she had been placed in a very unfortunate and uncomfortable position. Because of the staff's concern about her health issues, she had been moved to the open ward which housed both male and female patients, and her bed was immediately next to the nursing station, which offered absolutely no privacy. While this made good sense for staff to observe the patient, nevertheless, the lack of privacy and having males and females in the dormitory would have been extremely difficult for someone who appeared wary and on edge in an environment which she probably did not understand.

I was told her name was Santina, however, having a good awareness of Italian culture, when I approached her I addressed her as "Signora", rather than by her first name. I believed this would make it easier for her not to feel patronized. Referring to her as "Signora" provided her with a level of distance and, hopefully, a sense of security, as I was concerned that staff had been pushing her to do things like drinking and eating, and she was fighting against this. I also noticed that Santina had a set of rosary beads in her hand and she seemed to be moving her lips without making any audible sounds. I assumed she was reciting the rosary, which culturally, is done to pray for the dead, praying together as a family or a community, as well as privately, and when someone is going through a difficult time. It consists of a set of Hail Marys, and Our Fathers, recited over and over, a number of times.

In preparing to see if I could help encourage this woman to drink fluids, I asked the nurse to get a cup of water and place it near Santina's bed when I approached her. Then, I said in Italian, *"Signora! You are obviously very religious and you enjoy prayer. That is wonderful, as prayer helps you get close to God. You know, Jesus, the Son of God, was an important person and he taught us many things. Today it is very hot, and in many ways, in Jerusalem, where Jesus lived, he often had to travel to other cities. As you would know, Israel is a hot country and travelling from one city to another, Jesus would have to travel through the desert. As you can imagine, in the incredible heat of summer, Jesus needed water, otherwise his lips would be parched, and he wouldn't be able to reach the other city. Therefore, he would need to drink water: fresh water which is pure and healthy, to make sure that he would stay well and healthy. The heat of summer and the desert made it important for Jesus to ensure he drank plenty of water, regularly."*

At the end of this monologue, I apologized that I hadn't introduced myself earlier, and I explained that I worked at the hospital, that I spoke Italian, and that she could come and talk to me if she wanted. Santina stared at me rather diffidently, not responding verbally at all. After a minute or two, I excused myself and went through the ward to see another patient. However, over the next period, as the ward was open and there were no partitions, I occasionally glanced over towards Santina's bed. Each time I looked, she still appeared with rosary beads in hand, and sitting on the edge of her bed. Shortly before leaving the ward, I went to the nursing station to talk with the nurse who had asked me to see if I could help Santina drink. I said, *"I'm sorry. It seems that what I tried hasn't worked. I will attempt to come around later in the day and see if I can get through to Santina."* At this, the nurse responded, *"You're joking! She's had three cups of water since you left. It was amazing, because as soon as you left, she looked at the cup and drank all the water. I've just occasionally come to refill the cup and she had two other cups. It was amazing what you did. I don't know what you said to her, but whatever it was, it worked."*

I was pleasantly surprised, as I had thought that she hadn't drunk any of the water. Obviously, the story of Jesus and the desert seemed to touch Santina and stimulate her thirst, and she started drinking. Fortunately, this was helpful in getting Santina to drink regularly, and she also slowly started eating. Occasionally, I would pop in to the ward and casually come to where Santina was, and greet her. After about two days, in response to my greeting her by saying *"Ciao signora! How are you?"*, she said in Italian, *"Anyway, who are you?"* I told her my name, and I explained that I was a Clinical Psychologist and that I worked at the hospital. I also told Santina that if there was anything that she needed, to let me know and I might be able to help her. This didn't produce any further conversation. However, after another few days, when I was about to greet her, Santina said, *"So you're the psychologist, and you work here?"* I nodded and asked her if there was anything I could do for her. Surprisingly, she said, *"Yes"*.

She then added, *"I don't know why I am here and I don't like being here. But can you help me telephone my daughter as I haven't seen her for a long time?"* I said that I would do what I could to help her call her daughter. From her case notes, I also explained to her why she was in hospital and what needed to happen for her to reach a point where she could be discharged. This helped build a sense of trust with me, and she was able to speak with her daughter Sara, with whom she had conflict, which had actually resulted in this hospitalization. Santina's daughter attended a few joint therapy sessions, and slowly reconnected with her mother, and over time they were able to talk about the initial conflict situation and do what they could to resolve it. When Santina was discharged, her husband and daughter felt that Santina was emotionally better than she had been in years.

After discharge, with out-patient support, Santina was also able to connect with some Italian-community resources, which provided positive contact with people she felt comfortable communicating with. This helped her develop some significant friendships which Santiina needed, as Sara was in the process of leaving home. The initial family conflict revolved around Santina's distress at her daughter wanting to leave home. Having new friends with whom to converse and who could understand her culture and way of thinking helped Santina to more easily accept the normal developmental change of accepting Sara as a young woman, who needed to get on with her life.

In one of the family sessions, Sara reminded her mother that just as she had grown up and decided to leave Italy, against

Santina's mother's wishes, to get on with her life, the time had also come for Sara to leave her parents' home and live her own life, too. This gradually made sense for Santina, to the point that she was eventually able to give Sara her blessing to leave home.

The story of Jesus travelling through the desert became a minor legend at the hospital, and several times staff members reminded me of this. Towards the end of that summer, when it was still unusually hot, at a team meeting, the nursing staff provided background about a new patient named Cornelius, who had recently been admitted. He was a man in his sixties, who had trained to be a Catholic priest, without ever having been ordained. Despite this, he had spent most of his life connected with the parish priest of a suburban church, doing odd jobs, for which he received food and lodgings. He had a serious problem with alcohol, and he was diagnosed with Korsakoff's Syndrome. He was known at the hospital as he had had several previous hospitalizations. Recently, he had a psychotic episode, whereby the priest who looked after him was struggling to cope and eventually had him admitted.

When he was admitted to hospital, the staff were concerned as Cornelius had seriously harmed himself by running head-first into a wall causing bleeding and haematomas to his head. Due to his unwillingness to stop this behaviour, the staff then placed him in a padded cell to reduce the risk of further injury. However, they were then concerned about Cornelius urinating on the floor and then, kneeling and walking on his knees over the urine. The staff's attempts to prevent him from doing this wasn't very successful for the first twenty-four hours. After the first day in the padded cell, Cornelius refused to drink any fluids, which solved the problem of urinating on the floor. However, Cornelius' determined refusal to drink then created concern in the staff about his level of hydration as it was extremely hot both day and night.

Therefore, due to the popularity of the story of Jesus travelling through the desert, I was asked to see if I could also help this man drink water to overcome his dehydration. Feeling rather pleased with myself at the request, I agreed to see Cornelius with the nursing staff after the meeting. I saw him in the cell, together with the charge nurse and two other male nurses. As we entered the cell, Cornelius was lying on the floor, even though there was a fixed bench in the cell to sit on. The nurses had with them a plastic cup and a water container. The nurses, who were familiar with Cornelius, asked him to stand. He stood up and the charge nurse, who was also familiar with Cornelius, introduced me to him. This then gave me the opportunity to say how I appreciated being able to meet him. I also went on to say that I heard he had studied in the seminary and he had spent most of his life doing God's work.

With that I continued: *"And, as you know, Jesus was the son of God. Jesus lived in Judea, and in those times people travelled either by foot or on horse back or by donkey. When Jesus had to travel from one city to another, he often went on foot. In Judea, it was usually very hot. When Jesus travelled from one city to another he had to travel through the desert, which was very, very hot. Yes, hot, really hot! To make sure that he could get to the other city, he needed to make sure he had plenty of water. Water is essential to ensure we are healthy. Jesus would always bring plenty of water for him to drink during the hot journey through the desert. In his travel he would often stop to have a drink of some cold, pure water to restore his energy. In those days, it was very hot, just like it is very hot right now. And Jesus made sure that he had plenty of water to drink on his journey.'* With this, I ended my "sermon", and said goodbye to Cornelius, as I observed one of the nurses with a plastic cup of water proffered towards him. I then left the room, believing my job had been done.

From there, I went to a lunchtime meeting. Later that afternoon, I returned to the ward to see how everything had fared. The atmosphere on the ward was fairly quiet and flat. Obviously, as I had not seen or heard what happened after I left, I was surprised that none of the staff came rushing up to me to report the outcome. I eventually saw one of the nurses who was in the cell at the time, and approached him, asking him what happened. He looked at me, and then said, *"I think it's best for you to ask Chris."* Chris was the charge nurse. I was puzzled at this response. So I asked, *"Why do I need to ask Chris? Why aren't you able to tell me?"* Despite my question, I still received the same reply: *"You need to talk to Chris."* Therefore, I went around trying to locate Chris.

I'm not sure if it was intentional avoidance by Chris, or not, however, it took some time to locate him. When I did, I said, *"I spoke to Bruce about what happened after I left today with Cornelius. I asked him, but he insisted that I needed to speak to you about this. What happened?"* Chris, with a strange look on his face, first started to turn away, and then turned to me and said, *"So, you want to know what happened after you left?"* I said, *"Yes, what happened?"* At this Chris sighed, and then continued, *"Well, as you left I reached out and offered Cornelius a cup of water. He waited a moment, then he took the cup and slowly put it to his lips and looked at me. I waited for him to drink the water. However, at this point, he took the cup and threw it all over me."* I burst out laughing, and Chris said, *"Yeah, laugh why don't you! That's what the nurses did. But I was the one who copped a drenching. I don't think it was all that funny!"* At this, I apologized and agreed that it would not have been funny for him at the time.

In recounting this story, I realised that there were several issues which mitigated success in the one instance, and failure in the other. Obviously, while what you do in therapy works very well sometimes, unfortunately, that doesn't guarantee that simply repeating the same intervention in another situation is going to achieve the same result. This experience first with Santina and then with Cornelius demonstrated to me that it's not just the intervention or the technique which determines the success. It is not just what you do. It has more to do with what happens between the therapist and the client.

Somehow, with Santina, something happened that helped her be open to hearing me tell the story about Jesus and connect her with her thirst. It could have been my understanding about her culture: calling her "signora" rather than "Santina". This, I believe, was important, as in her culture it would be rude and patronizing for someone who is not her friend or equal, to call her by her first name. It could also have been just "good luck"! Another possible factor could have been that I spoke in her language. These factors, and the fact that I continued to visit her, without imposing myself on her, may have made it possible for her to start to trust me and talk to me about her daughter. In addition, I believe that as Santina wasn't pressured by me to drink the water, nor was she pressured by me to have to respond when I spoke with her, may have made it easier for her to hear me and eventually respond.

However, with Cornelius, I simply had a five-minute contact, with little connection. Also, you could assume that his Korsakoff's Syndrome may have also added to his inability to allow me to connect with him. It was more a "zip in — zip out" technique or intervention. I did little to form a therapeutic relationship with Cornelius, thereby not being able to influence him in any way. Therapeutic interventions on their own are *not* what make therapy effective. What is vital in therapy is the therapeutic relationship itself!

Chapter 8
The Peaches Were Delicious

Matteo was a strong, athletic man, who attended therapy with his family, and he made an instant impact when he said, *"If you're going to tell me what that dickhead at the hospital said, then, I'm going to leave straight away!"* With surprise, I asked, *"Who's the dickhead?'* Matteo said, *'That doctor dickhead from the hospital. He said that I can't hit my kids. He said that we had to come and see you. But if you're going to say the same thing, then I'm leaving and taking my family with me."*

The rest of the family looked uncomfortable and embarrassed. Mirella, the mother, then chimed in and said that their eldest daughter Serena had been admitted to the Emergency Department following a suicide attempt, and on discharge, the doctor had referred them for family therapy. Mirella was soft-spoken and very concerned about her daughter's safety. As brash and forthright as Matteo was, Mirella attempted to portray the compensatory level of due respect for professional status.

Serena, at seventeen, was the eldest of three daughters. She was an attractive young woman who only responded when asked a question and was also soft-spoken. Her sisters, Laura and Nina were fifteen and thirteen respectively, and were smaller and younger versions of Serena. In obtaining background information, all three girls were able to respond adequately to questions, but they often looked towards their mother or father when answering, appearing to check out whether their parents were accepting of their answers.

I told Matteo that I had no prior information about why they were referred, and I would appreciate understanding why they attended and what they would want from family therapy. As the initial session evolved, Matteo was able to provide a clear history of events that led to Serena being hospitalized following a drug overdose. The week prior to the overdose, Serena had been invited to a party by a girlfriend at school. Anticipating that she wasn't going to be allowed to attend, due to her father's strong cultural beliefs that girls can't go out unchaperoned, she approached her mother. Mirella, who was Australian-born of Italian parents, understood the difficulties of being a female caught between two cultures and was open to allowing Serena more freedom, but she found it difficult to argue with Matteo, who would become highly emotionally aroused when she disagreed with him, and he would start to shout and bang things.

However, as Serena was in her final year of high school, and Mirella wanted to trust her daughter, she agreed to talk to Matteo and try to convince him to let Serena go to the party. Despite Mirella's best efforts to convince Matteo to allow Serena to attend the party, Matteo insisted that she was not allowed, and he used the fact that she would be finishing high school soon and that he would reconsider the situation about Serena being allowed out on her own, after her final exams. When Mirella advised Serena that she was not allowed to attend the party, she tried to stress the fact that she believed things would change once she finished high school, hoping that this would soften the blow of disappointment for Serena. Mirella said that she thought this had worked, because Serena's reaction to not being allowed to attend the party was not as bad as normal.

Matteo and Mirella explained that Serena had not appeared unduly moody on the evening of the party. However, Serena had said that she was needing to study for the forthcoming final exams, and went to her room shortly after dinner. After about two hours, Mirella realized that Serena had not come out of her room, so she decided to check on her. Knocking softly on the bedroom door, Mirella finally entered the room to find it dark, and she was surprised that Serena was in bed. Unsure whether to check if Serena was asleep, she decided not to, and left the room quietly, to avoid disturbing her daughter.

After another hour, Matteo commented that he hadn't seen or heard Serena since dinner, and he wondered if she was okay. Mirella advised him that Serena was in bed and asleep, as she had checked on her earlier. Matteo expressed surprise, saying that it was unusual for Serena not to create a drama when she wasn't allowed to go to a party. This discussion encouraged Mirella to quietly re-enter Serena's bedroom and on checking again, she realized that the bed was made up with pillows to form the shape of her body. But Serena was not in the bed! Also, Mirella noticed that the bedroom window was fractionally open.

Being aware of this, Mirella was now in a great dilemma, not being sure what to do! Should she disclose the situation to

Matteo and then have to deal with an explosion by Matteo, as well as with his reaction to Serena when she would come home? Or should she just not say anything to Matteo, which might avoid all the angst that was likely to occur? However, if she chose not to let Matteo know, what would happen if he found out? Also, how would she feel about not being honest to her husband if she didn't tell him? With all these cascading and conflicting thoughts going through her head, Mirella finally decided that she needed to tell Matteo that Serena had sneaked out of her room and had probably gone to her friend's party. On hearing this, Matteo became enraged and started shouting threats of what he would do when Serena returned home. Gradually, Mirella was able to calm him and help him stop shouting, as the other girls were asleep. He quietened down to the point that he convinced Mirella to go to bed, and he said that he would stay up until Serena returned, promising not to overreact when Serena came home. They made an agreement that they would talk about an appropriate punishment with Serena the next morning.

After midnight, Serena returned and entered her room via her window. As she crept in, she quietly started to undress, and was about to get into bed, when Matteo entered her bedroom. Asking her where she had been, Serena denied going out and said that she had just gotten up to go to the bathroom. Knowing this was a lie, Matteo got angry and started to shout and eventually he hit Serena with his hands when she kept denying what she had done.

A struggle ensued, with Mirella rushing to Serena's aid, trying to plead with Matteo about their agreement not to do anything until the morning. In the process, Matteo had hit Serena several times, and eventually Serena ran from her father to the bathroom, locking the door behind her. Although Matteo chased after his daughter, when she locked the door and he couldn't get in, with Mirella's pleadings, he was able to calm down sufficiently to stop shouting. With this, Mirella took over, trying to reason with Serena to come out of the bathroom. In the process, Mirella also had to calm and reassure Laura and Nina, who had woken to this middle-of-the-night racket. Once able to convince the younger daughters to go back to bed, Mirella resumed her attempts to prise Serena out of the bathroom, reassuring her that nothing would happen until the morning.

Regardless of her reassurances, Serena refused to respond in any way. Although this helped Mirella feel that things had calmed down, nevertheless, with time, Mirella became more and more anxious about the silence from the bathroom. She eventually spoke to Matteo, who had gone to bed, to see if he could get the door of the bathroom open, as she was concerned that there was some "pills" in the bathroom, and she hoped that Serena wasn't stupid enough to do anything silly.

Continuing to speak and trying to reason with Serena, eventually Mirella and Matteo decided that they needed to break into the bathroom. Following verbal threats by Matteo that he would break down the door, he eventually banged and punched holes in the door, to the point that he was able to get his arm inside, and unlock the door. There, slumped on the ground, was Serena! Attempts to bring her to consciousness were only partially successful, and after an urgent telephone call to the "Poisons" section of the hospital, they were advised to take her directly to the Emergency Department, together with anything they could find to assist the staff in clarifying what drugs she may have taken. This was followed by an inordinately long wait in hospital. Fortunately, it appeared that she had taken a cocktail of anti-depressants and sleeping tablets prescribed for Mirella, as well as a few analgesics, which, even all together, were not sufficient in number to be of long-term harm to her.

The following day, the hospital psychiatric consultant took a history, and Mirella said that he *"read the riot act to Matteo, saying that in Australia it was a crime to hit your kids, and that Matteo and his family needed to attend family therapy."* Apparently, Matteo argued with him, saying he was the father, and insisting that he could discipline his daughter anyway he wanted, which provoked an angry response from the doctor insisting that Matteo had a serious anger problem, and that if his daughter was ever to be admitted to this hospital for the same reason, the doctor would personally lodge a statement of assault against him. Thereby they were referred to me at the Multicultural Psychiatric Centre for family therapy as they were "ethnic".

Obtaining this information took up most of the first session. As Matteo attended ready for a "fight", expecting that I would take the same stance as the hospital doctor, I explained that I wanted to help them as a family, therefore I wasn't there to tell him what he could do and not do as a father. I didn't have much time left in the session, but I said that I would like all of them to come to a future session, where I would be able to provide them with relevant feedback on how I saw their situation, and my ideas on what I might be able to offer that could be helpful to them as a family. Mirella was quite anxious for the whole family to attend as quickly as possible as she was preoccupied with the fear of Serena's suicide attempt and how to handle not only what happened, but what she and Matteo could do in a similar situation of stress.

We were able to arrange an urgent appointment within a few days. Despite my attempts to avoid focusing on whether a father has the right to hit his daughter or not, Matteo still seemed obsessed with this issue, insisting on bringing this up several times during the second session. While the issue of violence in the family is of utmost importance in family therapy, my first focus on this family was to see if I could develop a rapport, a trusting therapeutic relationship, with each member of the family, and especially with Matteo, whose active involvement in therapy was crucial for me. Following several astute attempts by me to move away from this dead-end position, the issue of the importance of physical punishment to discipline children came up again. Matteo said, *"Look! There's nothing wrong with physical punishment. It doesn't do any harm. It helps to teach you what is right and what is wrong. My father loved me, and he used physical punishment and it didn't do me any harm!"*

In exploring this line of discussion, I asked him how he knew that his father loved him. Matteo said that his father showed it in many ways: by doing things for him, supporting him, teaching him work-related activities, and in many other ways. He also went on to say that he grew up in Southern Italy and came to Australia as a young adult. However, when he was about fifteen years of age, during a very hot summer, he and a friend were walking from the town centre to his home, which was a kilometre or two from the town. On the way, they went past the orchard of a neighbour who had the town's most delicious peaches. As he and his friend were hungry and thirsty, they looked around to see if the neighbour was to be seen. Thinking that the coast was clear, Matteo and his friend climbed the fence around the neighbour's property and took several of the most ripened peaches. They then found a shady place to stop to enjoy these delicious peaches.

Unbeknown to them, the neighbour had seen them stealing the peaches, and that afternoon went to tell Matteo's father about what his son had done. Later that day, when Matteo returned home, his father called him to go down to the "cantina" because he needed him there. On entering the cantina, Matteo described seeing a wooden bucket filled with water, and a thick rope dangling from inside the bucket. He also mentioned that there was another rope hanging from the rafter of the cantina. At first, Matteo didn't understand why these things were there. He asked his father why the ropes and bucket were there, but his father said that it didn't matter. He then told Matteo to undress. When Matteo objected, his father insisted and told him not to question what he wanted Matteo to do.

Matteo stated that at this stage he emotionally panicked. He couldn't understand what his father was doing and why. Upon being totally naked, Matteo was told to lie down on the ground, whereby his father tied the rope that was hanging from the rafters to his feet. As he did this Matteo said that he was crying and asking his father why he was doing this. He said his father paused, and said, *"What did you do today?"* To which Matteo replied, *"I didn't do anything!"* At that point Matteo said his father started pulling the rope that was draped over the rafter and raised Matteo by his feet off the ground. Matteo said that by this time he was hysterical and pleaded with his father to let him down. Matteo's father raised him a little higher and then tied the end of the rope to a ring that was concreted to the floor, leaving Matteo suspended upside down, held by his ankles.

At this point Matteo said that his father stopped and again asked, *"What did you do today?"* Again, Matteo replied, *"I didn't do anything!"* Matteo then said that at this point his father took the other rope that was hanging in the bucket full of water, swung it over his shoulder, and then struck Matteo on his back, as he was dangling from the rafter. Before each stroke he asked Matteo, *"What did you do today?"* After several strokes over his back, Matteo eventually disclosed that he and his friend Carmine had stolen some peaches from the neighbour. After one more stroke across his back, Matteo's father stopped, put down the wet rope, and said to Matteo, *"Don't you ever steal or take anything that is not yours! Never do that again!"* He then untied the end of the rope holding Matteo upside down, and slowly lowered him. He then untied his ankles and told him to dry himself and get dressed.

As Matteo was telling the story, I was aware that all the family members weeping and reaching out for tissues to mop the tears away. Matteo's eyes were watery right through this recounting. We paused at this stage to acknowledge the intensity of what he had just disclosed. In a soft voice I then said to Matteo, *"So you learnt a lot from this? Is that right?"* Matteo said, *"You bet I did!"* I then said, *"And you were clear that your father loved you?"* Matteo said, *"Yes, I was!"* I then asked, *"Now, tell me! When your father had you suspended in the air, and he took the wet rope out of the bucket and swung it over his shoulder, about to strike you with it, where was your father's love?"* Matteo replied, *"I don't know what you mean."* I repeated, *"When your father had you suspended in the air, and he took the wet rope out of the bucket and swung it over his shoulder, about to strike you with it, at that point, where was your father's love?"* Matteo looked astonished, not knowing how to respond. I repeated, *"At that point, when your father was about to lash you with the rope, where was your father's love?"*

Matteo hesitated a moment and then said, *"I don't know. I was just shitting myself. I was terrified and I'm sure I had pissed myself and shat myself from the fear!"* I said, *"So at that time, while you knew that your father loved you, the love wasn't there. You couldn't feel any love at that moment. All you could feel was intense fear from someone that you believed loved you, but the love wasn't there at the time!"* After another pause, Matteo said, *"Yeah! I guess so. At the moment I thought he was going to kill me. That's all I felt!"* I asked, *"So at that time, love didn't compute. All you experienced was extreme fear and helplessness?"* *"Yeah, I guess so,"* he replied, with an unusual look on his face. Becoming aware of this, I asked Matteo, *"You seem surprised somehow at all this. Can you help me understand what has happened as you were describing this?"* Matteo, much more open emotionally than he had been up to now, responded, *"I have never thought about that in this way. I think I just understood something just now."* At that moment he looked towards Serena. Until then his wife and daughters had been silent spectators to this intense disclosure. Everyone's eyes were watery, very much affected by Matteo's story.

"*Your look towards your daughter, what does it mean?*" I asked. "*What do you mean?*" was Matteo's reply. I answered, "*Your look towards your daughter Serena just now, what did the look mean?*" Matteo paused, and then he said, "*I suddenly realised that Serena probably doesn't understand how much I love her, even though I have tried to do the best I could as her father.*" I said, "*That's amazing! Say that again!*" Rather surprised, Matteo said, "*I don't know what you mean by amazing, that's just what I became aware of.*" "*Yes, that's fine. However, just say again, what you said just now, this time to Serena. Tell Serena what you realized about the 'love'.*" Matteo cleared his throat, paused and then looked at Serena, who had tears in her eyes, and said, "*I'm sorry that I haven't been able to show you how much I love you. A lot of the time I seem to be telling you what you can't do, and I just realized that you probably haven't felt the love I have for you.*" The tears in Serena's eyes became a waterfall and she started sobbing and her mother went over to her chair to hold her and cuddle her.

With this, Matteo's body language changed, and he seemed to stiffen and look away from his daughter. Noticing this, I said to Matteo, "*Matteo, say that again. Tell your daughter about the love you feel towards her.*" With this, Matteo, wiping away tears, again cleared his throat and said, "*Serena, you are my … our eldest daughter. Mum lost a baby before you came along, so when she was pregnant with you, we were both incredibly anxious. So, when you were born, and we saw that you were perfect, you were just so precious to both of us, and I remember how hard it was for me to get to sleep after we put you to bed. I just wanted to make sure you were okay and that nothing happened to you. You were our perfect child! I loved you so much!*" At this point I added, "*And let Serena know about your love for her now.*" Matteo cleared his throat, and continued, "*Serena, I love you now as much as I did the day you were born. I love you dearly!*"

The session ended shortly after this, but not before Mirella was also able to express her deep love for Serena, as well as her love for the other daughters who were involved in the session, even though they had said very little. From this session, it became quite clear that this family was "in *therapy*", and further sessions revolved around issues of culture and gender, negotiating age-appropriate freedom, responsibility, and trust. With Serena being seventeen years old, she needed to be able to navigate her way through life to feel normal compared to her Australian friends, as well as to value and to honor her Italian cultural roots. Issues of trust and freedom were important aspects that we focused on in the following sessions, as well as some couple work that Matteo and Mirella asked for, to help them communicate better and for Mirella to have a greater "voice" in the family, so that she didn't stay in the position that she had previously been in, of not having a voice in her family of origin, and again of not having a voice as a wife and mother in the current family.

The work which revolved around Serena, was also of great value for her two sisters, Laura and Nina, as the loosening up of rigid boundaries and the encouragement of negotiation between Serena and her parents made it easier for Laura and Nina to have a voice in the family, too. Although traditionally, it would have been easy to challenge Matteo's violent discipline of his daughter, from the outset, I believed that this would have precluded the possibility of providing anything useful to the family. It was a risk to avoid direct confrontation of his violence; nevertheless, when clients first attend therapy, the most important thing for me to do is to create a rapport with the client. If I join the client, then the client may join me!

This was a wonderful opportunity to work with a family, where the father was considered violent, rigid, and controlling; and yet, we were able to find a different route to a positive end of journey, rather than getting Matteo to attend "Anger Management" classes. My concern was that if I challenged him at the start, he would have been shamed for what in his mind was his way of being a good-enough parent. Matteo's story of the delicious peaches was a wonderful entry into family healing and family growth.

Chapter 9
Unbearable Anxiety

Nick rang for an urgent appointment. He explained to my secretary that he had been to see me with his family some years earlier, and he was struggling with anxiety. When we met, he asked whether I remembered him and his family. Although it was nearly ten years since I last saw him in family therapy, I remembered him and his family very well, as I had also seen his mother many years before that, when she initially attended with her siblings. At that time, Nick's mother, Irena, had come with her three brothers to decide about how best to support their mother who had been diagnosed with Alzheimer's. They were struggling to work together in deciding what to do for their mother. Irena was the youngest sibling, and being female, was treated by her three brothers as if she didn't really understand much, despite the fact that she was the one who was most actively involved in caring for her mother. Through the family therapy sessions, Irena was able to stand up for herself to demonstrate her knowledge, ability, and strength in confronting her brothers about having been patronized for many years. Irena's brothers, to their credit, were able to acknowledge this and eventually supported her suggestions about how to best provide for their mother's well being in her final years.

At his first appointment, Nick, a handsome young man about thirty years old, reported that he had been plagued with intrusive thoughts and unbearable anxiety over the last few months. It had reached a point that he was struggling to face each day. Nick worked in a family business which included his brother and sister, as well as both parents. Each of the family members had their area of responsibility, and although their father, Giovanni, had said ten years ago that he would retire from the business within a year or two, he was still actively engaged and unable to relinquish control of the family business. Irena and Giovanni had brought their family to family therapy when Nick was in his late teens, because all three children had entered the family business, and all three had difficulties working with their father who was very controlling, as well as being highly reactive emotionally when they did things which he didn't agree with.

Apart from Irena's role as mediator in the family, of the three children, I remembered Nick being the one who tried to mediate between his father and brother, and his father and sister. I also recalled that Nick played down his own frustrations with his father's idiosyncrasies.

Knowing this family background made it easier for me to have an awareness how the family operated and the various dynamics between the family members. From Nick's description of his workplace, it seemed that Irena still kept a part-time involvement there, primarily acting as mediator to ensure that she was available to palliate the situation and also be there for her children, if Giovanni got too stressed and put pressure on any of them.

However, in exploring the issue of intrusive thoughts and anxiety that Nick experienced, the family business did not appear to be a major factor. Nick said that he didn't know why, but in the last few months, he started to have intrusive thoughts which he couldn't shake off. Nick and his wife attended a gym, and there was a young female personal trainer who worked there. At odd times he found himself having intrusive thoughts about this young woman.

Nick acknowledged that she was very attractive, but he had no sexual desires regarding her. He was very distressed that these thoughts would surface without any reason, and at odd times. Nick was open with his wife Gloria, whom he loved very much, and told her of these thoughts, largely to reassure her that he had no desire to be with this young woman. He stated that he had been together with Gloria for almost ten years, and married for four years. Nick believed that they were close, and there was no question about his fidelity. Also, Gloria was very understanding about his situation and had been supporting him through this period.

Nick also said that he had experienced several panic attacks, in which he became short of breath, his heart rate skyrocketed, and he felt as though he was going to die. These episodes occurred at various times, and he could not understand why they had begun. On a recent occasion, he was at work serving customers, and he felt there was nothing to be stressed about, and suddenly, he experienced a severe panic attack; he had to stop working and eventually after a few hours, he drove home, as he could not settle sufficiently to continue working.

Nick stated that he had been to see his family doctor, who did the necessary tests, and ruled out any other possible cause apart from anxiety. The doctor prescribed a mild tranquilizer and another medicine to take the edge off his anxiety. Also, apart from referring Nick to me, the doctor suggested that he focus on his breathing if he felt another panic attack come on. Whilst Nick knew that the doctor was trying to help him, he couldn't understand how the breathing would help, as he just went into panic and felt he couldn't control his breathing when the panic came on. Nick was hopeful that coming to see me would help him, as he didn't want to become reliant on drugs to control what he was feeling emotionally.

Nick was a deep thinker. In summarizing his symptoms, he said that the intrusive thoughts started before the panic attacks. However, he now realised that any time that he had a panic attack and needed to stop what he was doing, he found that the intrusive thoughts became even more prominent. Nick also said that his panic symptoms now stopped him from working and concentrating on what he was doing, thereby giving him more time to think, and then the intrusive thoughts became even more intense. He just wished they would go away. Nick had debated what to do about the intrusive thoughts, including staying away from the gym so that he didn't see nor have any contact with the young woman. However, Gloria felt that he didn't need to do that, as she trusted him implicitly.

I asked Nick to help me, by letting me know what factors he had considered might have been associated with these events. Whilst his first response was *"Nothing!"*, I asked again to tell me what he had considered, even if he wasn't sure. With this, Nick said that his workplace was still stressful. He felt that he could handle it; however, he only had Monday off, and worked 60–70 hours each week. He knew that this was not good, but he was used to it, and he didn't let his father's stress affect him most of the time. However, Nick was concerned about the lack of common time he and Gloria had together. She had been working Monday to Saturday, and had Sundays off, whereas he had Mondays off. They spent time together in the evening, but he never got home before 7 pm; two or three evenings a week they went to the gym, often together. Nick was concerned about the lack of quality time together. He was also concerned that Gloria had recently left her job because she wasn't happy, and she was about to start a new job, which he believed Gloria would find difficult, as she didn't handle change well.

Another factor that Nick believed could have been part of the onset to these problems, was his preoccupation with trying to research real estate, as he and Gloria wanted to find an old house they could buy, and then demolish the house to use the land to build their dream home. For several months he had been researching real estate to the point of exhaustion, and he felt that he had run out of steam to continue doing the research thoroughly. Nick and Gloria had also been talking about when to get pregnant, as they both wanted children. Nick's biggest worry was not being able to realise his plan which involved first locating a house to buy, designing their dream home, then building their home, and, then, once their "nest" was set up, eventually getting pregnant. In the last few months, with the anxiety and intrusive thought problems, Nick just didn't have the energy to keep exploring the real estate market, and he was distressed about falling behind in his quest. He also prided himself as someone who achieved results, and he was very self-critical at his inability to overcome his symptoms and resume his task of locating an old house for their dream.

At the end of the first session, I outlined what I could assist him with. To overcome Nick's anxiety symptoms, I suggested that he could use any relaxation or meditation methods that he already knew. If he had not previously learnt any methods, I could provide some relaxation CDs which he could listen to at home, and I could then help him employ the relaxation to overcome the anxiety symptoms. I also wanted Nick to explore both the anxiety symptoms and the intrusive thoughts, as well as what these meant. Based on the information he provided in the first session, I felt that he needed to review what was happening in his life, and not just try to obtain symptomatic relief. Therefore, it was important to explore both the anxiety and the intrusive thoughts, symptomatically, as well as their underlying issues. Nick was happy to do this work, and left the session together with a set of relaxation CDs that he agreed to listen to.

At the next appointment, Nick said the week had been up and down. He felt that having seen me and being able to say openly what was happening in his life had been helpful. He was happy that he had been honest and had said what he had said, rather than worrying about what he should say, in case I thought badly of him. I asked what might I have thought badly of him, and he said about the intrusive thoughts. Nick was worried that I might think that he had "bad" thoughts about this young woman, but in disclosing his intrusive thoughts to me, he felt accepted and valued, rather than judged in any way.

The "down" involved the fact that he had continued to have periods where he was fine, and then out of the blue, he started having anxiety symptoms. The thing he found most difficult was that he couldn't understand why these feelings suddenly arose and why he couldn't control them. Nick prided himself with the belief that he could think things through, and work most things out in his mind. However, ever since these problems started, he felt out of control, almost as if he had lost his ability to be in control of himself. Also, when he felt the anxiety symptoms, he had to stop what he was doing and then, the more he thought, the more the intrusive thoughts would arise. He asked whether the intrusive thoughts represented unconscious desires or wishes that he was not aware of. Could it be that he had unconscious desires to be with this young woman, or was it something else? This was all too confusing for him!

Nick also said that he had started to listen to the relaxation CDs and he could relate to them. Whilst he had never done any meditation, he thought it would be useful for him to learn to meditate, as he could understand how this could be useful in his life. He felt that although he couldn't fully put the relaxation into effect yet, he had started to focus on the breathing when he experienced anxiety symptoms, and it seemed to slow down the symptoms and they didn't last as long. Nick felt hopeful that the relaxation training would be helpful for him and he would continue to use it.

Nick also wanted to talk about the fact that Gloria was so supportive, that he felt truly blessed in having her as his wife. He said that they had a very strong relationship and each had supported the other throughout the time they had been together. Nick believed that one of the factors which had contributed to his current problems was the fact that he had become so focused on the material things in life, working hard to build a wealth base, trying to purchase a block of land to then build a dream home, whilst losing track of the importance of the special relationship he and Gloria had. In his reflections between sessions he realised that the symptoms were telling him that he had lost balance in his life, and that both he and Gloria needed to look at their lifestyle and plan a better way of being there for each other and spending quality time together. I was pleasantly surprised to hear his reflection on his presenting problem. From initially believing that he had this *"terrible thing growing inside him"* and wanting someone to help him remove this growth, to now starting to recognize that he had to listen and understand what these symptoms were telling him about his life and lifestyle, this was marvellous progress.

At various times during the early therapy sessions, I suggested that he invite Gloria to a session so that she could provide some input which might help me understand things from her point of view. Although Nick didn't oppose the idea, nevertheless, there were several reasons why she couldn't attend. Gloria had just started a new job and he said that she found it difficult to ask for time off from work. Also, he was getting a lot out of the sessions, and he felt he was making progress. Therefore, Nick continued to attend on his own and continued to vacillate, at times stating that he was making progress and being able to implement the relaxation and breathing to deal with his anxiety symptoms, and at other times, still being frustrated at not being able to be in total control of his symptoms.

He started to reduce his time at work, and told his father that he needed to look after his health and well-being more. His father seemed not to have any problem with this, which somewhat surprised Nick. However, he thought that his mother must have had something to do with this, as he had expected his father to complain and make it difficult for him to reduce work.

At about the sixth session, Nick reported that something incredible had happened for him. He had a sales order to deliver in the city, so he decided to leave work early to do the delivery, so that he would then go home early and spend some time with his wife. He said that ordinarily, he would have worked to the last minute, then gone to make the delivery, ending up getting home late.

Nick said that he arrived in the city around three o'clock in the afternoon. As he was about to enter the building to do the delivery, he saw a young man lying on the pavement at the entrance to the building. He paused to observe the young man, and then entered to deliver the goods. On his way out, Nick noticed that the young man was still lying on the pavement, and people walked past him, not appearing to notice him. He debated what to do, and then decided to approach the young man. After starting to speak with him, Nick sat next to the young man and continued to talk. At first the young man hardly responded to Nick. Nonetheless, Nick persevered with his conversation, and gradually the young man, who said his name was Brett, started to tell Nick about the fact that he was a psychiatric patient and he had attempted suicide on several occasions. Brett told Nick that he had no family and that his father had deserted him at an early age. His mother died of a drug overdose, and he had lost touch with his older sister who had left home many years ago.

Nick spent the next two hours conversing with Brett. They talked about many things, and Nick said he didn't quite know how they went from one conversation to another. They talked about Brett's background, his struggle with wanting to live, the current political situation, about humanity, and many other issues. Nick was amazed at the level of human contact he experienced in those two hours with Brett. He became acutely aware of how we, as human beings, generally avoid human contact. Nick said that through this experience, he became acutely aware that although hundreds of people passed by this young man lying on the pavement, it was almost as if the young man didn't exist. During the two hours that Nick sat next to Brett and talked to him, only one other man came to check if they were okay. Nick was overwhelmed with the thought that although we are human and we say that we are social beings, yet we are so disconnected with ourselves and immersed in what we are "*doing*" that we are not at all in touch with other human beings.

After a couple of hours, Nick said goodbye and asked Brett for a hug. They both became very emotional at this very meaningful, physical, human contact. Nick eventually drove home in what he described as an elated emotional state. He said that this experience with Brett helped him feel something he hadn't experienced for quite some time. In fact, from my understanding of Nick's journey, it probably helped him more than anything that we did in all the therapy sessions. He felt alive and glad to be alive. He could see that this young man had serious mental health problems, and at the same time, Brett was more alive and *"in touch"* than a lot of other *"well"* people. Nick realized that just stopping to speak with Brett and being in the present, helped him notice that he needed to listen to his body and what it was telling him.

Nick arrived home considerably later than he had planned that day, but when Gloria saw him arrive, she noticed something significantly different about him and she shared the joy and excitement that he was experiencing when he described his meeting Brett. She was pleased at the change in Nick, and they experienced the best evening together that they had had for some time.

From this experience, Nick became more secure within himself. While he continued to attend therapy, there was considerably less urgency in having weekly sessions, and the gap between appointments grew to several weeks. Nick eventually arranged for Gloria to accompany him to an appointment. While Gloria described herself as an introvert, she nevertheless handled the session in an easy and relaxed way. She appeared very supportive of Nick and believed that he would get through this period. Gloria acknowledged that through this difficult time, both she and Nick had needed to talk about emotional things, which they had not done for some years. She also knew that they needed to reassess where they were going in their marriage, so that they could ensure that they stayed together emotionally. All in all, partly by chance, and partly by Nick's decision to share his humanness with Brett, Nick found a path to self-healing and dealing with his anxiety and panic issues which could have continued overwhelming him, for a long time.

Following the one session with both Nick and Gloria, I received several telephone messages and emails to say that Nick was handling his anxiety symptoms sufficiently well, and he didn't feel the need to attend therapy any more. Nick also said that the intrusive thoughts had paled into the background. Nick and Gloria felt they were closer than they had been for some time, and Nick said he was appreciative that his anxiety and intrusive thoughts had helped him to review what was most important to him: *"being together in a loving relationship"*.

Nick's story highlights how in therapy clients can start from a position of fear and helplessness, not knowing how to deal with their plight, and eventually reach a place of strength and resourcefulness. The therapist's contribution is important in achieving progress; however, there are also other factors outside the therapy room which contribute to the progress. In this case, seeing Brett and taking the time to talk to him, when others shunned and avoided this dishevelled young man lying on the ground, was a significant factor in Nick's improvement. This significant human encounter helped to open something in Nick which then triggered his own healing qualities. Nick's story attests to the healing qualities each of us have within.

Chapter 10
I Keep Thinking of Ways to Murder Him!

Mojgan rang for an urgent appointment, saying that she and her husband Ahmed, needed help with their marriage. She said that they had reached a crisis in their marriage and unless they got help, she couldn't stay in the marriage. When they arrived for their first appointment, Mojgan, a very attractive woman in her mid-thirties, and Ahmed, a tall, handsome man, about the same age, were very pleasant and appreciative in obtaining this appointment at such short notice. They were both of Persian background, arriving in Australia as children, and doing their schooling in Australia. Both seemed very warm people, who became positive and connected when they described their two sons aged six and eight. However, when I asked about the reasons for attending therapy, they became critical, negative, and blaming of each other.

Mojgan opened the session saying that she and Ahmed had a Love-Hate relationship. When asked to explain what this meant, she said that she was clear that they loved and cared about each other, however, in the blink of an eye, they could go from being loving and affectionate, to tearing strips off each other emotionally. Mojgan said that whilst in the first few years of their marriage they argued a little, particularly about who was right and who was wrong, these arguments were insignificant, compared with the last three or four years. She said that their current arguments had become totally overwhelming, and she had reached the point that unless they made significant changes, she would divorce Ahmed.

Ahmed listened to his wife's description of the presenting problem, and while he didn't verbalize anything, his body language spoke volumes. His body movements and occasional sighs and head rolls were indicative of the fact that he disagreed with most of what Mojgan outlined. When I asked Ahmed to describe the reasons for attending therapy, he stated that it was true that now they were arguing regularly, and he couldn't sleep at night due to the arguments; however he added, *"To have an argument it takes two people!"* He said that Mojgan was simply blaming him for the arguments, and she would not take any responsibility for her part in them. Also, he was frustrated that in recent times, she used the "Divorce Card". When I asked what the Divorce Card meant, Ahmed said, "*That as soon as I raise something that she doesn't like, she immediately threatens divorce. This is frustrating, and I want this to stop!*"

In getting background history from them, both Mojgan and Ahmed said they were born in Persia, and their families came from the same city. Each arrived in Australia within months of the other and although the families had not known each other in Persia, both sets of parents had met through their ethnic community connection in Australia. Growing up, the two families had occasional contact and Ahmed made friends with Mojgan's older brother, Mustafa. Through this friendship, Ahmed said he watched Mojgan grow and blossom into a woman, and he maintained the friendship with Mustafa, primarily to be able to see Mojgan and talk to her from time to time. Mojgan was also attracted to Ahmed, and in their late teens, they disclosed their attraction and love for each other. For some time they kept this secret; however, when Mojgan became concerned that Ahmed was doing little to approach her father about marriage, she put pressure on him, and Ahmed finally got the courage to speak with her father.

Ahmed said that despite his apprehension at approaching her father, he was surprised that when he finally plucked up the courage to speak to him about marrying Mojgan, her father wasn't effusively happy to give his blessing. Ahmed said, "*It wasn't that he was negative about me marrying Mojgan, it's just that I expected him to be overjoyed and happy for us to get married. Instead, he talked about how important it was to think things through, because marriage was a serious issue, and he wanted me to think about it and come back to discuss it in a month.*" From Ahmed's description, this already started to create a gap between Ahmed and Mojgan's father. Despite initially perceiving her father as a strong patriarch, Ahmed started to feel that he wasn't going to be accepted as a "son" by him.

After a month, Ahmed arranged to meet Mojgan's father and said that he was adamant that he wanted to marry Mojgan. By this stage, Ahmed had completed his degree at university and had a good, well-paid job, and felt he had all the credentials to marry his daughter. Yet, whilst Mojgan's father agreed to their marriage, the engagement was long and tortured for Ahmed. It took several years for them to get married, and her father was very strict about set customs, especially for girls, and they were only allowed to go out either as a family, or with a chaperone: usually with Mustafa. Ahmed found this difficult, as growing up in Australia, he wanted to do things with Mojgan on their own, and to get to really know her, rather than always to have someone in the family present with them. Also, he felt stymied sexually. Both he and Mojgan wanted to develop a sexual relationship, but this was extremely tricky when others were always around. Mojgan also wanted more freedom from her family; however, being raised with certain beliefs and values, she struggled to oppose her father's wishes, and often tried to placate Ahmed when he became frustrated.

After several years' engagement, the two fathers got together and agreed about how the wedding should be done. Both Ahmed and Mojgan stated that the wedding went well and at last they could start a life together. By this time Mojgan had also completed her university studies and was working in a full-time job. Together they planned a life with joint dreams and goals. They bought a house prior to their wedding, and decided that they would wait a few years before having children. They first wanted to establish a secure base before raising a family. They described this early stage of their life together as happy, connected, with the two of them working together. They were both respectful of the other's families and had regular contact with both families. They also felt they could have quality time as a couple, travelling and enjoying joint activities, including concerts, theatre, and entertainment. They described this period as the best part of their marriage. Although they initially had difficulties conceiving, after several months, and first researching potential medical assistance to facilitate conception, Mojgan spontaneously got pregnant and then had their first child: Stefan. They described him as a *"Wonder Child"*. They said that the pregnancy was unremarkable, and the birth was a magical experience for both of them, despite being hard work for Mojgan. They felt blessed with this wonderful child.

Around the time of the pregnancy with Stefan, Ahmed had become disenchanted with his work. He felt that he wasn't challenged in his work, as well as not being valued by his employer. Ahmed talked to Mojgan about resigning from work and setting up his own business. This troubled Mojgan, as she believed this was not the time to make such a huge change. Being pregnant, she was anxious about the fact that she would soon be stopping work and their income would reduce. Also, she toyed with the idea of not returning to work after the birth, and becoming a stay-at-home mum. She tried to talk to Ahmed about these concerns, but he was insistent about his needs, and Mojgan felt dismissed and insignificant. Then, at the beginning of the third trimester, with little notice, Ahmed resigned from his job to set up his own business. Mojgan was furious with him. How could he do such a thing without having her agreement! She cited this issue as a deep wound which had never been dealt with. She felt that this was the beginning of Ahmed simply looking after his own needs, and not considering her. Also, she mentioned that this was the time when she noticed that Ahmed *"always"* wanted to have the last word in any argument.

Nevertheless, despite the volume of work and energy needed in setting up his business, Ahmed made sure that he was there for Mojgan in late pregnancy and also for Stefan, once he was born. Despite Mojgan's fears about the financial risk involved with setting up a new business, Ahmed seemed to have the magic touch, as the business took off financially, and before long she started to feel more secure financially. As the business grew, Ahmed took on new staff members, which in turn, helped the business to grow. After eighteen months, the business was well established and Mojgan asked Ahmed to consider if her brother Mustafa could also be given a job. Initially he wasn't happy with this idea, so he listed a number of factors which he believed mitigated against having his brother-in-law join the business, including the complication of having family members involved as employees, as well as Mustafa's personality, which Ahmed struggled with. Despite these concerns, as Mojgan kept insisting that Ahmed employ her brother, he eventually acceded to her wishes, and employed his brother-law.

Ahmed described this period as difficult. He found that Mustafa struggled against taking orders. In the business, there was a lot for Mustafa to learn, as it was not work that he was familiar with. Although he was an intelligent man, he would often say that he knew what to do, even if he had never done a particular job previously. Mustafa believed he could pick things up easily, and Ahmed started to get frustrated at not knowing how to approach his brother-in-law and get him to do the job properly. Each day Ahmed would return home and most of his discussions with Mojgan revolved around his frustrations with Mustafa. This became difficult for Mojgan, as she felt like the meat in the sandwich. She was aware about some of the personality flaws that her brother had, and the fact that Mustafa believed he knew everything. At the same time, this was her brother, and often she found herself defending him. These arguments created a further rift between Ahmed and Mojgan.

To add insult to injury, Mojgan's father then spoke to his daughter, to convince Ahmed to employ her younger brother Mozzafor, as well. This became another stumbling block for the couple, and their arguments increased. However, because of the strong family ties that both held dear, Ahmed again reluctantly bowed to Mojgan's wishes, and Mozzafor was also employed. Following this, whenever they argued about anything, Ahmed would always bring up this issue of how he had given in to her and to the wishes of her father.

Nevertheless, in the first session they both agreed that despite these issues, there were also good times during this period, and the birth of Marcus, their second son, brought them close. They were delighted to be blessed with a good second pregnancy and a relatively easy birth. They were happy with their two sons, and despite the family politics, the business was thriving—until one day, when Mustafa asked to speak with Ahmed about changing the business relationship from employer-employee, to business partners. At first Ahmed was shocked, and didn't quite know what to say. To have time to think, he said he would give it some thought and then get back to him. As had happened previously, the more time elapsed, the more he felt pressured by Mojgan to allow her brother and his family to benefit from the business. Eventually, Ahmed said that he *"caved in"* and reluctantly agreed to this change.

As bad a decision that it may have been, Ahmed had no idea of what was to come. Now that Mustafa had a share of the business, he started to make moves to have a bigger say in the decisions of the company. Ahmed started to feel increasingly disenfranchised by Mustafa's decisions, which he started to make unilaterally. Having Mozzafor join the company wasn't such a problem; Mozzafor actually seemed to get on better with Ahmed than with his own brother. Mozzafor often gave Ahmed support, which Ahmed had not expected. However, about a year and a half after Mustafa became a director in the business, and had assumed control of the Accounts section of the company, he had given Ahmed some documents to sign, and without realizing it, Ahmed had signed a document which made him personally liable for a loan that the company had taken. Unfortunately, the economic climate changed, and they lost several contracts. Due to the loss of several contracts, the lending institution wanted the loan repaid.

Eventually Ahmed became aware of this treachery by his brother-in-law and confronted him with the deception. Mustafa denied that he was responsible for any deception, and insisted that the decision was made by Ahmed to take full responsibility for this loan, and the company was not liable. Ahmed was furious at Mustafa and couldn't believe that he could do such a thing, not only to him, but also considering that it also affected his own sister and her family. Ahmed became so incensed that he threatened to take legal action against Mustafa. Mojgan became distressed at the thought of this becoming public and pleaded for him not to do this to her brother, convincing Ahmed to go to her father and ask him to mediate.

Once Ahmed was able to calm down, he agreed to see Mojgan's father and disclosed what Mustafa had done, believing that his father-in-law, being the elder in the family, could then resolve the matter in the best way possible. To his amazement, his father-in-law chose to say that as both he and Mustafa were adults, he was not going to take sides, and that Ahmed needed to resolve this directly with Mustafa. With this, Ahmed felt doubly betrayed by both his brother-in-law and his father-in-law. He lost all respect for Mojgan's father and from there the arguments between Ahmed and Mojgan escalated.

At home, Ahmed would fluctuate from being deeply depressed to flying into a rage. At night he was unable to sleep, and the couple were in regular conflict. Although he sought legal advice, eventually, because of the family ties, Ahmed decided not to follow through on legal action. Over time, and with a professional mediator, Ahmed agreed to cut his losses, and eventually turned the company over to his brother-in-law, losing more than a million dollars. Although at a head level, he knew this was the best way of extricating himself from such an untenable position, emotionally he was a mess. He agonized over how stupid he had been to agree to all the demands of his wife to allow her scheming brother to enter the business and eventually steal the business from him. He deeply resented his father-in-law for not intervening and disciplining Mustafa for the injustice he had done to Ahmed and Mojgan. Ahmed strongly believed that it was his father-in-law's duty to intervene and shame Mustafa for committing such a scurrilous act against Ahmed and his own sister.

At the end of the first therapy session, both Mojgan and Ahmed agreed that they wanted to work at improving their relationship to ensure a healthy future for their two boys. They both said they would work at reducing their arguments and they wanted help with being able to communicate better with one another. Mojgan said that she wanted Ahmed to stop reacting and blaming her for what her brother and father had done. Conversely, Ahmed wanted Mojgan to stop jumping to divorce talk, as soon as he expressed anything that she didn't like to hear.

In giving them feedback, I was troubled at their focus on blaming the other. This usually results with a bleak prognosis for improvement in a relationship. The two need to focus on their own change, rather than trying to change their partner. Therefore, I told them that I was concerned that their level of motivation to take responsibility to change their own behaviour was low and that this did not auger well for therapy. I impressed upon them that although I was prepared to work with them, nevertheless, I would require both to show their level of commitment by making changes to their *own* behaviour. If they continued therapy with me and strayed from putting effort into personal change, my job would be to keep them on track. They listened, and at least verbally, they both agreed that they would welcome this, and they said that they would each focus on their own personal changes in the ensuing therapy.

From that session on, they attended weekly. They fought, they argued, and they also started to make changes. When they argued, I kept raising the fact that they had two children who were six and eight, and they were both adults in their thirties. Yet, from their description, when they argued in front of them, *their children became the adults, and they were operating as two-year-olds!* This stung them both, to the point that they gradually reduced their level of arguments in front of the children. However, in the middle of the night the arguments continued. They described situations where they would work together in the evening and create a good environment for the boys. However, once they went to bed, things changed. Often, they would start being close and loving, however, invariably, something would happen during their lovemaking, that would end up with one or the other saying something that brought her family into the bedroom, and their lovemaking just fizzled out. This had been happening for some time and they struggled with what they could do to prevent this pattern continuing.

At the sixth session, Ahmed attended on his own, saying that Mojgan had to take her mother to hospital and was unable to attend the session. He had discussed with Mojgan about still attending on his own and she was agreeable to this. Ahmed wanted to talk about the fact that he couldn't sleep at night and he wanted help to change this. He went on to remind me that often their lovemaking was cut short due to one of them bringing up something about Mustafa or Mojgan's father. Ahmed said that he would then end up not being able to sleep all night. Also, at other times Ahmed would go to bed and try to sleep, however, Mustafa's image would come up in his mind, and he would regurgitate every damaging things Mustafa had done to him, ending up with Ahmed tossing and turning all night. Ahmed explained, *"When this happens, I keep thinking of ways to murder him! He has destroyed my life, my peace and my happiness. He is the worst possible representation of a human being! He is a worm. No human being could do such a thing to his own family!"*

When I asked Ahmed what he meant by thinking about ways to "murder" his brother-in-law, he said, *"Oh, I know that I wouldn't do it. I want to be there for my kids. If I did murder him, that would be great to pay him back for the harm he's done, but my kids are more important."* I was pleased to hear that it was just fantasy and Ahmed was not planning to follow through on his fantasy. I therefore said, *"So it seems that you must really love your brother-in-law!"* Ahmed looked at me astonished. He paused and then said, *"Are you joking? What do you mean by that?"* I responded, *"Well, despite what he's done, you won't let him go. You keep him close to you, even in bed."*

Disbelieving, he said, *"That's weird. I detest him. He's the lowest form of life. I hate his guts and I won't go to any family event when I know that he'll be there. If I could exorcize him from my life I would do it.'* I replied, *"Well, I understand that you hate him and want to cut him out of your life, nevertheless, you continually carry him around wherever you go, including taking him to bed with you."* I then went on to say, *"Ahmed, would you do something with me? Would you come to the kitchen with me?"* Rather surprised, he nodded, and we went into the kitchen. I took two water glasses from the cupboard. I then asked Ahmed to wait for me, while I went outside to gather some dirt, sand, dead leaves, and other fine rubbish, and returned to the kitchen. I then poured water into one of the glasses, and said, *"Water is the source of life. It is essential to our being. We need water and pure water to stay well and healthy. However, in life sometimes things happen which are crappy and unhealthy."* At this point, I took the sand, dirt, rubbish and decayed material I had gathered outside, and poured it into the glass containing the water, and with a tea spoon, stirred the mixture together, and then offered it to Ahmed saying, *"Here drink this!"* At this he drew back in surprise, not knowing what to say. After a further pause, I said, *"You know that although we want things to always go the way we want, shit happens, and we just need to suck it up. Here, drink this, it's just like what you've been doing for some years, sucking up what your brother-in-law has been giving you, and you've taken that with you to bed, while you're making love, and when you're relaxing. Everywhere you've gone, you've sucked it up, so don't worry about it. Just drink this!'* After a further pause, his body language changed, and Ahmed stood taller and said, *"I've never thought of it that way. I've always thought about this as being that I can't get away from him, rather than that I keep carrying him around with me!"*

With this, I nodded. I searched for two coffee filters, and said, *"Come here, Ahmed."* I walked over to where the two glasses were, and took the empty glass and placed one of the coffee filters over the glass, and then poured the contents of the other glass into the filter. The water went through the filter into the empty glass. While the filter withheld the sediment, it allowed the water to pass. The water in the second glass was slightly coloured, but was clear of the junk and slime that the filter retained. I then said,

"Sometimes things happen that are not healthy and that we don't want. When that happens, we need to filter out the toxic parts, even though we can't totally control everything." Then I took the clean filter, and gave it to Ahmed and said, *"Here, take this filter. Place it on your bedside cabinet, and whenever it is time to go to bed, pick it up and remember to use this to filter out any shit or toxic stuff that you've absorbed, or that starts to go through your mind. Also, use it if you start to sleep and a thought or dream interferes with your sleep and you start thinking about all the old shit that you no longer need. Use the filter to get back the essence of life and health."* With this, we ended the session.

At the following session Mojgan attended and remarked that since the last session they had experienced the best two weeks for a long time. Ahmed had told her about the water and the filter, and he had been using it. Mojgan acknowledged that she needed to help Ahmed by staying focused on being there for him and with him. She realized how much she had also contributed to the decline in their sex life. Mojgan said that she could now see how committed Ahmed was to the therapy, and this awareness had made a huge impact on her. She felt much more committed now, especially as she could see the progress that they were making.

In the remaining sessions we focused on their re-establishing better communication as well as learning to resolve conflict. Their commitment to being parents was instrumental in helping them develop the skills to stay "adult" when they argued, rather than regressing into childish arguments and tit-for-tat sequences. Mojgan and Ahmed said they wanted to model better communication skills for their sons. They subsequently included the boys in a therapy session. The family session with the boys was extremely helpful, because both Ahmed and Mojgan were able to talk to the boys about what they had been trying to achieve through therapy. Both sons had a really good idea about the emotional status of their parents and when they were asked if there was anything they each wanted to say to their parents, they both expressed deep concern about the parents' well-being and their relationship. This surprised Mojgan and Ahmed, as they had thought that they had been keeping things from their kids. Also, the boys remarked how much better it had been for the last month. They were aware that something had changed for their parents, and they wanted this change to continue. This gave

Mojgan and Ahmed further motivation to continue the good work they had started.

Before ending the sessions, Ahmed and Mojgan agreed to perform a ritual, in order to lay to rest the hurts and wounds that each had experienced over their time together. In preparation for this ritual, I suggested that they write down all their hurts and resentments, which had often been expressed when they had previously gotten into emotional turmoil. Also, I wanted them to each write down what they wanted to ultimately achieve in their relationship as a couple and as parents. They needed to describe not only what they wanted, but what they would do to ensure that they achieved this new level of relationship. Then they could decide on a special day when they could do this ritual. In further preparation, they needed to go to a nursery and buy a plant that they both liked, a plant which represented life, energy, and vitality: The sorts of things they wanted in their life together!

I asked them to set a date for this ritual. At the appointed time they were to locate a suitable place in their garden, and there dig a hole. Once done, they were to read their lists of hurts and wounds they had accumulated over time, and when finished, place the two lists in the hole. Then they were to pour some soil over the hurts and wounds which they wanted to lay to rest. I then asked them to read out the things they wanted in the future, including what they would commit to do to achieve these things. Once completed, they would then place the plant in the hole, pour soil around the plant to ensure a firm base, and then water the area around the plant. Then each day, as they watered the plant, they would also be able to symbolically remember to nourish their relationship, both as a couple and as parents. Mojgan and Ahmed both liked the idea, and in due course, performed this ritual to lay the past to rest and focus on a new future. At the end of therapy, they both reported a good level of improvement in their relationship and the hope that the progress was to be well grounded and consistent.

In Ahmed and Mojgan's story, although they started as complainants, each blaming the other, my role as a therapist was to be honest and confront them with my concerns about this, to guide them and help them stay focused on what they could each do to change. I clarified my role and how I would work with them at the outset. Although they both said they wanted change, in the early sessions both Mojgan and Ahmed regularly reverted to their "default" position of blaming the other. However, with constant reminders, restraints, and blocking from me, they were gradually able to make the shift, and focus on their own ability to change themselves. This important change in Mojgan and Ahmed was instrumental in their making significant progress in their relationship, both as a couple and as parents. Helping them to open their eyes to a different view, helped each to make significant change. Also, once one started to make changes, this helped the other to engage in making changes, as well.

The individual session with Ahmed and confronting him with the "jarring" concept that he was *keeping* his hated brother-in-law and father-in-law in the marital bed, rather than Ahmed believing that he had no ability to control the thoughts of these two people, worked well. Ahmed also responded very well to using the coffee filter. Also, over time, Mojgan and Ahmed's strength and resourcefulness to make changes showed through, and their children benefitted from these changes. Working with this family was a great pleasure and it gave me hope that regardless of how entrenched problems are, with effort and commitment to change, progress is possible.

I sincerely hope you have enjoyed these stories.

About The Author

Clinical Psychologist Aldo Gurgone is a well-known Australian relationships therapist. He has been practicing family therapy since 1972. His experience and background in family therapy spans work in Australia, the UK, Italy, Malaysia, Singapore, and Peru. Aldo continues to provide individual, couple, and family therapy as well as Clinical Training and Supervision of Mental Health Professionals and Agencies. Aldo provides therapy for individuals, couples, and families who attend for a wide range of health-related reasons.

Over the years, Aldo trained with several of the pioneers of Family Therapy including Virginia Satir, Carl Whitaker, Lynn Hoffman, John Weakland, as well as a number of second generation Family Therapists, including Maurizio Andolfi. His professional background includes experience in a Therapeutic Community in England in the late 1970s, as well as working in a range of Psychiatric and Multicultural settings. He enjoys the blend of working with clients, conducting training courses, seminars, workshops, and supervising.

www.ingramcontent.com/pod-product-compliance
Lightning Source LLC
Chambersburg PA
CBHW040136270326
41927CB00019B/3401